D1743169

Spanish Grammar for Beginners

A Step-By-Step Approach to Learn Spanish <u>FAST</u>

This Complete Spanish Grammar Guide Will Teach You to Speak Spanish With Confidence & Ease
(Vol. I)

By: World Travel Institute

Table of Contents

Introduction

Spanish, or *español*, is a beautiful language that can be very difficult to master. Still, according to research trajectories, by 2050, there will be 754 million Spanish-speakers in the world. Whether you're traveling to South America, studying in Spain, or wanting to explore Spanish culture, this is the book you've been looking for. With *Spanish Grammar for Beginners*, you'll have access to the ultimate Spanish guide with tons of relevant and helpful tips and user-friendly instructions to study and learn Spanish—fast!

By using this guide, you can expect to perfect your Spanish speaking, writing, and reading abilities. From understanding grammar to common phrases to memorizing dates and times and mastering the infamous conjugations, *Spanish Grammar for Beginners* will be your #1 resource in your Spanish-learning journey.

This guide features a vast selection of enhanced and detailed lessons that will improve your Spanish skills right away. In just a short time, you'll obtain great knowledge over Spanish syntax, vocabulary, and expressions. And the more you delve into this book, the more you'll learn about the different parts of speech, such as Spanish nouns, articles, adjectives, adverbs, and pronouns, in addition to routine interactions that you'll experience both at home and abroad.

Within days, by trusting this guide, you'll build the confidence and ability to walk into a Peruvian restaurant to order *un café*, navigate through the metro in Málaga, find a hotel in Mexico City, and wander through any Spanish-speaking region in the world. *¡Bienvenido a la lengua española!* Welcome to the Spanish Language!

Chapter 1 - Spanish Grammar: Understanding Parts of Speech

1.1 Nouns

Nouns are words that name and identify people, objects, settings, animals, concepts, and things. For example, "car" is a noun. "Joseph" and "candle" and "capitalism" are all nouns. Similar to English, Spanish nouns can come in different forms. Nouns can be singular like *perro* (dog) or plural like *botellas* (bottles); additionally, nouns can come in three distinct forms in both languages: common nouns, proper nouns, and compound nouns. Still, while both languages share grammatical similarities, there are a few major differences between Spanish and English nouns. First, we will address the comparable forms of nouns.

Types of Nouns

Like stated previously, both Spanish and English have three distinct forms of nouns.

Common Nouns: Nouns that name people and things, such as *libro* (book) and *mamá* (mom). These nouns do not get capitalized in a sentence.

Proper Nouns: Nouns that name specific individuals, locations, and places. For example, Gabriel García Márquez, *las Montañas de Los Andes* (the Andes Mountains), and Santiago de Chile. Generally, proper nouns are capitalized in both Spanish and English, but there are some differences to this rule in Spanish. Languages, demonyms, religions, days, and months are not capitalized in Spanish, as they would be in English. Some examples include *miercoles* (Wednesday), *mayo* (May), *el ateísmo* (Atheism), and *el idioma italiano* (the Italian language).

Compound Nouns: Two or more nouns combined together to name and identify one object or person. In Spanish, the main noun is always mentioned first, and it's followed by the attributing or a supplemental noun. This differs in English, where the attribute is placed before the main noun. For example, *Las Tierra de Fuego* (The Fire Lands) is a compound proper noun that includes the main noun (the lands), as well as the attribution (of fire). In both Spanish and English, you will encounter common nouns turned into compound nouns, i.e., *la estación del tren* (the train station).

The table below includes additional examples of Spanish nouns:

Common	Proper	Compound
el libro (the book)	*España* (Spain)	*el mar Caribe* (the Caribbean sea)
el bebé (the baby)	*Malága* (Malaga)	*la Ciudad de México* (Mexico City)
el parque (the park)	*El Prado* (The Prado)	*la Plaza de Mayo* (the May Plaza)

Turning Singular Nouns Into Plural Form

In Spanish, similar in English, nouns can come in amounts. That's to say that nouns can be singular or plural. Spanish plural nouns will almost always end in *–s* or *–es*. It often depends on the final letter of a word. For example, *el carro* (the car) is a singular noun, where in comparison, *los carros* (the cars) is a plural noun.

If a singular noun ends in a vowel (a, e, i, o, u), add an *-s* to the end to make it plural. The table below includes some examples:

Singular	Plural
el gato (the cat)	*los gatos* (the cats)
la tarjeta (the cards)	*las tarjetas* (the cards)
la planta (the plant)	*las plantas* (the plants)

If a singular noun ends in a vowel plus a consonant, a vowel plus "y," or a vowel plus "ch," add -*es* to the end to make it plural. The table below includes some examples:

Singular	Plural
el color (the color)	*los colores* (the colors)
el planeta (the planet)	*los planetas (the planets)*
el año (the year)	*los años* (the years)

Understanding Gendered Nouns

Like most Romantic languages, but differing from English, all Spanish nouns have a gender. This means that all Spanish nouns are either feminine or masculine. It's important to differentiate whether a noun is feminine or masculine because it will impact the construction of a sentence. For example, *el sol* (the sun) is a masculine noun, meaning that the articles and adjectives that will accompany the noun must also be masculine: *El sol es amarillo.* (The sun is yellow).

Unfortunately, there is no formula to determine whether a noun in English will translate into a feminine or masculine Spanish noun; thus, the best way to recognize whether a noun is feminine or masculine is to observe a noun's ending. Almost always, feminine nouns end in −*a* or −*ora*, while masculine nouns end in −*o* or −*or*. (You may have noticed, from the examples above, that the article "the" also changes form in Spanish, depending on the noun that follows it.) Take a look at the table below for further examples:

feminine Nouns	Masculine Nouns
la mujer (the woman)	*el hombre* (the man)
la taza (the cup)	*el doctor* (the doctor)
la cama (the bed)	*el cuadro* (the picture)
la computadora (the computer)	*el calendario* (the calendar)

Of course, as rules go, there are always exceptions; in the case of Spanish nouns, there are some nouns that, while having a certain final letter, won't have the expected gender. Again, discerning how to tell a Spanish noun's gender is complicated, and it is best to memorize the nouns in their entirety, rather than guessing the gender when translating from English. The table below features some Spanish nouns that break the rule:

feminine Nouns	Masculine Nouns
la conversación (the conversation)	*el agua* (the water)
la canción (the song)	*el poema* (the poem)
la mano (the hand)	*el policía* (the police officer)
la radio (the radio)	*el problema* (the problem)
la moto (the motorcycle)	*el tequila* (the tequila)

1.2 Pronouns

Pronouns are words that refer to the participants in a sentence or to someone or something else mentioned in a sentence. Examples of pronouns include "I," "You," "We," and "They." In the sentence, "Luis and I drove from Málaga to Seville," the word "I" is a pronoun that indicates the subject speaking. In Spanish, pronouns are used similarly to how they're used in English; in other words, pronouns serve to clarify and stress the subjects in a phrase.

The Personal Pronouns in Spanish

The following table indicates all the pronouns used in Spanish, as well as example sentences to complement their usage:

Subject Pronouns	Example Sentence
yo (I)	*Yo estoy bien.* (I am fine).
tú (you)	*Tú estás bien.* (You are fine).
él/ella (he/she)	*Él está bien. Ella está bien.* (He is fine. She is fine.)
ustedes (you - Plural)	*Ustedes están bien.* (You all are fine.)
nosotros (we)	*Nosotros estamos bien.* (We are fine.)

An important note to make is that the plural form of "He" and "She" (*ellos* and *ellas*) utilize the same verb conjugation as *ustedes*. There will be more about verb conjugation in the following section. For example, in the phrase *Ellas están bien, y ellos estan bien*, it's important to distinguish the similarity between the verb *están* in this example and that of *ustedes*.

Omitting the Subject Pronouns

Similar to other Romantic languages, in Spanish, speakers can exclude the subjective pronoun from a sentence. This can occur because conjugated verbs indicate who or what is the subject of the expression. For example, rather than saying *Yo estoy bien*, the subjective pronoun *yo* can be omitted, leaving the sentence as *Estoy bien*, which is grammatically correct and the most common form of speaking and writing in Spanish. The table below will illustrate other examples of excluding the subject pronoun:

Subject Pronouns	Example Sentence
yo	*Estoy emocionado.* (I am excited.)
tú	*Estás emocionado.* (You are excited.)
él/ella	*Está emocionado. Está emocionada.* (He is excited. She is excited.)
ustedes	*Están emocionados.* (You all are fine.)
nosotros	*Estamos emocionados.* (We are excited.)

In other cases, the subjective pronoun can be omitted, depending on its placement in a sentence or connecting sentences. For example, the following table will depict two related sentences:

> *A mi novia le encanta viajar. Está en la ciudad de Puerto del Rosario en España.*
>
> (My girlfriend loves to travel. She is in the city of Puerto del Rosario in Spain.)

The sentence above, and other with this form, allow for the subjective pronoun to be excluded because the first sentence establishes the subject, and the second sentence follows the same subject. Of course, whether someone chooses to omit the Spanish subjective pronoun or not, pronouns are incredibly important parts of the Spanish sentence, and their usage will continue to evolve in the coming sections.

1.3 Verbs

Verbs are words that describe an action, state, or circumstance. For example, "run" is a verb. "See," "hear," "transformed," and "is" are all examples of verbs. Just like in English, Spanish verbs can come in various styles. However, in Spanish, verbs take on different forms, depending on the context of the sentence; this is known as the conjugation of verbs. While conjugating verbs may seem like the most challenging part of learning Spanish, the following grammar rules will alleviate any stress and confusion.

Infinitives, Finites, & Conjugation

In Spanish, verbs come in two distinct forms: infinitive form and finite forms, also known as the conjugated form. Spanish verbs end in *–ar*, *–er*, or *–ir*. For example, *guardar* (to save), *correr* (to run), and *decir* (to say). This verb form is designated as "infinite" because they are not anchored to a time or place. When the infinite form is conjugated, the verb becomes the finite form because it refers to an event or circumstance with a certain tense: past, present, or future tense. For example, "I ate an apple" is past tense; "I am eating an apple" is present tense; "I will eat an apple" is future tense."

The table below breaks down the many forms a verb can take in Spanish, depending on perspective: first-, second-, or third-person perspective. They also depend on the number of speakers — singular or plural. The following table will use the verb *mirar* (to watch), a word ending in –*ar*, as an example:

Mirar	
yo (I - Singular)	*miro*
tú (you - Singular)	*miras*
él/ella (he/She - Singular)	*mira*
ustedes (you - Plural)	*miran*
nosotros (we - Plural)	*miramos*

As demonstrated above, to conjugate Spanish infinitive verbs that end in –*ar*, just drop the –*ar* and replace with either –*o*, –*as*, –*a*, –*an*, or –*amos,* depending on who and how many are speaking. Below, you will find another table that illustrates how to conjugate *comer* (to eat), a Spanish infinitive verb that ends in –*er*, and *vivir* (to live), another verb that ends in -*ir*:

Comer		Vivir	
yo	*como*	*yo*	*vivo*
tú	*comes*	tú	*vives*
él/ella	*come*	*él/ella*	*vive*
ustedes	*comen*	*ustedes*	*viven*
Nosotros	*comemos*	*sosotros*	*vivimos*

As it's shown by the table, to conjugate –*er* infinitive verbs, you replace the ending syllable with –*o*, –*es*, –*e*, –*en*, and –*emos*. In the case of infinitive verbs ending in *–ir*, the final syllable changes to *–o*, *–es*, *–e*, *–en*, and *–imos*. Of course, these conjugations pertain to Spanish infinitive verbs in the present tense. Past and future tenses require different forms of conjugation; but, with the tables below, memorizing all kinds of conjugations will be greatly simplified.

Past & Future Tense Conjugations

To describe the appropriate conjugations of the different Spanish verbs, the following verbs will be utilized as examples: *hablar* (to speak), *beber* (to drink), and *dormir* (to sleep):

Hablar			
Past Tense		**Future Tense**	
yo	*hablé*	*yo*	*hablaré*
tú	*hablaste*	*tú*	*hablarás*
él/ella	*habló*	*él/ella*	*hablará*
ustedes	*hablaron*	*ustedes*	*hablarán*
nosotros	*hablamos*	*nosotros*	*hablaremos*

Beber			
Past Tense		**Future Tense**	
yo	*bebí*	*yo*	*beberé*
tú	*bebiste*	*tú*	*beberás*
él/ella	*bebió*	*él/ella*	*beberá*
ustedes	*beberión*	*ustedes*	*beberán*
nosotros	*bebimos*	*nosotros*	*beberemos*

Dormir			
Past Tense		**Future Tense**	
yo	*dormí*	*yo*	*dormiré*
tú	*dormiste*	*tú*	*dormirás*
él/ella	*durmió*	*él/ella*	*dormirá*
ustedes	*durmieron*	*ustedes*	*dormirán*
nosotros	*dormimos*	*nosotros*	*dormiremos*

It's evident in these tables that whether a Spanish infinitive verb ends in *–ar*, *–er*, or *–ir,* most of the conjugations in the past and future tense overlap with one another. Of course, while there are a few infinitive verbs that break the rules, the great majority of verbs follow the grammar rules. Therefore, while verb conjugation may seem like a massive mountain to climb, by following the rules illustrated in this chapter, conjugation will quickly become second nature.

1.4 Adverbs

Adverbs tend to have different purposes. Generally, adverbs are words that modify or qualify how frequently something happens, where it happens, and when it happens. These kinds of words tend to express circumstances regarding a setting, time, degrees of occurrences, and so forth. For example, "inside" is an adverb that details a place; "often" is an adverb that illustrates the frequency of an occurrence; "recently" is an adverb that clarifies a time. In both Spanish and English, adverbs provide greater depth to sense structure. Spanish adverbs, just like Spanish verbs, must be conjugated to fit the context of a sentence. There are three distinct ways to conjugate Spanish adverbs: adding – *mente* to feminine adjectives, by integrating nouns with a Spanish preposition, and, lastly, by memorizing certain Spanish phrases commonly used as adverbs.

Adding −mente to Adjectives

The two-syllable −*mente* is the Spanish twin of the English adverbs that end in -ly. Because adverbs are different from adjectives, which need to be in gender and numerical agreement when describing a noun or pronoun, adverbs don't need to be in agreement with the verb they detail. The table below demonstrates how to conjugate feminine adjectives and turn them into Spanish adverbs:

Adjective	feminine Form	Adverb
rápido (fast)	*rápida*	*rápidamente* (quickly)
lento (slow)	*lenta*	*lentamente* (slowly)
primero (first)	*primera*	*primeramente* (firstly)
nervioso (nervous)	*nerviosa*	*nerviosamente* (nervously)
cansado (tired)	*cansada*	*Cansadamente* (tiredly)

Adding -*mente* to a feminine adjective is the most common way to conjugate Spanish adverbs; still, there are two more ways of doing so.

Integrating Nouns With a Preposition

In certain instances, adding −*mente* to a feminine adjective may result with an awkward-sounding adverb. In other circumstances, certain adjectives lack a feminine form, for example, *respeto* (respect) and *difícil* (hard). When these cases arise, a way to conjugate an adverb is to add the preposition *con* (with) to the noun to form an adverbial expression; these phrases take the purpose of a single adverb. The table below illustrates how to add *con* to a noun to create a Spanish adverbial expression:

Noun	Adv. Expression (Con + Noun)
paciencia (patience)	*con paciencia* (patiently)
tristeza (sadness)	*con tristeza* (sadly)
energía (energy)	*con energía* (energetically)
respeto (respect)	*con respeto* (respectfully)
madurez (maturity)	*con madurez* (maturely)

This form of Spanish adverbs is also common, considering that there are a few adjectives that lack a feminine form. In those cases, here's the way to work through it. Still, there remains one more way to conjugate a Spanish adverb.

Memorizing Spanish Adverb Phrases

Certain adverbs in English don't have Spanish counterparts. For example, there is no one word Spanish equivalent for "finally," "willingly," or "immediately." Instead, Spanish speakers have adopted adverbial phrases to describe certain adverbs. The table below offers the most commonly used Spanish adverbial phrases:

Adverbial Phrases I	Adverbial Phrases II
más tarde (later)	*tan tarde* (so late)
a veces (sometimes)	*por supuesto* (of course)
ahora mismo (now)	*de repente* (suddenly)
de nuevo (again)	*con despacio* (slowly)
de vez en cuando (infrequently)	*muy poco* (very little)

hoy día (nowadays)	mientras tanto (meanwhile)
todos los días (everyday)	al fin (finally)
más lejos (further away)	en seguida (immediately)

By utilizing these three methods, conjugating adverbs will become yet another important tool in your Spanish arsenal. These three methods will guarantee that any adverb fits accordingly to your messages, both verbal and written.

1.5 Adjectives

Adjectives are descriptive words used to express the forms, styles, colors, sizes, and speeds of nouns, and verbs. In other words, adjectives are the spices that elevate sentences to be more concise, eloquent, and vibrant. Adjectives are pivotal building blocks in all languages; especially in Spanish, adjectives bring a necessary flare to the tongue. Similar to adverbs, adjectives are also responsible for clarifying and characterizing people, objects, places, and actions. And just like verbs and proverbs, Spanish adjectives must also be conjugated to fit the context of a sentence. The following grammar rules will facilitate the conjugation process, as well as outline the placement of adjectives in Spanish.

The Agreeing Adjective

In Spanish, most adjectives are placed after the noun they're modifying rather than before the noun. For example, in English, the phrase "The red dog" would be *"El perro rojo"* in Spanish. Take notice that the adjective *rojo* comes after the noun, not in front of the noun. Additionally, Spanish adjectives need to agree with the noun's gender and number; to adjust adjectives into their required form, it's necessary to conjugate them into their masculine or feminine forms and make the adjective singular or plural. Thankfully, all the conjugations rule from before are the same for conjugating adjectives. To further explain the concept, the table below will feature the proper conjugations for *frio* (cold):

Adjective	feminine Form	Singular	Plural
frio (cold)	*fría*	*Una tarde fría.* (A cold afternoon)	*Unas tardes frías.* (Some cold afternoons)

In most cases, to turn an adjective into its feminine form, the only necessary step is to replace the *−o* with *−a*. Additionally, to turn an adjective into its plural form, all that's required it to add an *−s* to the final syllable. More examples can be found in the table below, which include some very common Spanish adjectives:

Adjective	feminine Form	Singular	Plural
divertido (fun)	*divertida*	*Una noche divertida.* (A fun night)	*Unas noches divertidas.* (Some fun nights)
pequeño (small)	*pequeña*	*La camisa pequeña.* (The small shirt)	*Las camisas pequeñas.* (The small shirts)
lindo (pretty)	*linda*	*Una gata linda.* (A pretty cat)	*Unas gatas lindas.* (Some pretty cats)
malo (bad)	*mala*	*La mañana mala.*	*Las mañanas malas.*

		(The bad morning.)	(The bad mornings)
rápido (fast)	*rápida*	*La niña rápida.* (The fast girl)	*Las niñas rápidas.* (The fast girls)
nuevo (new)	*nueva*	*Una blusa nueva.* (A new blouse)	*Unas blusas nuevas.* (Some new blouses)
lleno (full)	*llena*	*La casa llena.* (The full house)	*Las casas llenas.* (The full houses)
viejo (old)	*vieja*	*Una taza vieja.* (An old mug)	*Unas tazas viejas.* (Some old mugs)

Most Spanish adjectives follow the conjugations rules visualized above. As stated previously, it's important for an adjective to have the corresponding form to match the noun it is describing. Of course, per previous grammar rules, the conjugation of adjectives is not consistent because there are some adjectives that break the rule and have their own specific forms. But, the adjectives are easier to memorize, and there are four distinct types to know.

Exceptions to Adjective Conjugation

The Spanish adjectives shown here do not change in form, either for masculine or feminine forms or for singular or plural use. The adjectives who break the conjugation rules fall into four categories: adjectives ending in –*e*, adjectives ending in consonants, adjectives ending in –*ista*, and, comparative adjectives that end in –*or*. The table below offers adjectives that fall into these categories. Once again, keep in mind that these adjectives are not to be conjugated, and they retain their original form:

End in -e	End in Consonant	End in -ista	Ending in -or
amigable (friendly)	*azul* (blue)	*pianista* (pianist)	*mejor* (better)
verde (green)	*gris* (gray)	*alarmista* (alarmist)	*menor* (less)
grande (big)	*atroz* (atrocious)	*extremista* (extremist)	*superior* (superior)
triste (sad)	*marrón* (brown)	*periodista* (journalist)	*inferior* (inferior)

Conjugating adjectives should be a lot more painless with these easy-to-remember rules. By accumulating these conjugations on top of the ones previously explored, properly matching adjectives to their corresponding nouns will become elementary.

1.6 Articles

Articles are words that have only two functions: 1. To present a noun; 2. To indicate the gender (feminine or masculine) and number (singular or plural) of a noun. In English, the most commonly used article is "the." However, in Spanish, articles change in form depending on the context of a sentence. In general, there are two types of articles: indefinite article and definite articles. The difference between both classes depends on how specific the article is. For example, *unos* (some) is indefinite, while *el* (the) is definitive. The following section will illuminate the ways to differentiate between the two kinds of Spanish articles with eas.

Understanding Indefinite Articles

In Spanish, just like in English, indefinite articles have four major purposes: to highlight a quantity in the plural, to describe specific qualities of a person, to clarify a noun that is not well-defined, and with the verb *hay* (there is). There are four forms of *un* (a), which will be displayed in the table below. The table also shows the four ways to use an indefinite article:

Singular Masculine	Singular Feminine	Plural Masculine	Plural Feminine
un (a)	*una*	*unos* (some)	*unas*
To Describe	**To Clarify**	**To Quantify**	**Hay**
El niño es un príncipe. (The boy is a prince.)	*Mariel es una compañera de Mari.* (Mariel is one of Mari's co-workers.)	*El hotel está a unas 12 millas de aquí.* (The hotel is some 12 miles from here.)	*Hay unas frutas en la mesa.* (There are some fruits on the table.)

Just like definite articles, indefinite articles are prominent in both verbal and written Spanish. Conjugating either form of article will only become easier in time and with constant practice.

Understanding Definite Articles

Definitive articles are everywhere, and in Spanish, just like indefinite articles, definite articles come in four forms, and, additionally, definite articles serve many functions in Spanish. The table below will illustrate the forms, as well as common uses:

Singular Masculine	Singular Feminine	Plural Masculine	Plural Feminine
el (the)	*la*	*los*	*las*

Specify Noun	Specify Title	Specify a Family	Specify Time
El aeropuerto está muy lejos. (The airport is very far away.)	La Presidenta Luna vive en la capital. (President Luna lives in the capital.)	Los Gacías son personas amables. (The Garcias are kind people).	Son las 3:30 de la tarde. (It's 3:30 in the afternoon).

There are other uses for definite articles, for example, to specify a weekday: *El viernes es un feriado* (Friday is a holiday). Another usage is to refer to geographical features, such as mountains, lakes, oceans, and seas: *el océano Atlántico* (the Atlantic Ocean); *el mar Mediterráneo* (the Mediterranean Sea); *el río Rinca en España* (The Rinca river in Spain).

Of course, as previously demonstrated with grammar rules, there is one exception to article forms. And that would be when articles and prepositions blend together.

A New Splice: Article + Preposition

In Spanish, like other Romantic languages, certain phrases are shortened to save time and letters. In this case, the article *el* (the) combines with *a/de* (to/of). A direct English translation doesn't exist, so it will require a bit of time to get used to this phrasing. In the long run, however, this combination saves time. The table below will demonstrate the two possible combinations:

A + El = Al	De + El = Del
Yo quiero ir al cine. (I want to go to the movie theater.)	*Ese carro es del abogado.* (That is the lawyer's car.)

Articles are necessary staples of Spanish grammar; with these simple rules, Spanish articles will become another important asset of a Spanish learner's language ability and skill.

1.7 Conjunctions

Conjunctions are words that connect two words, connect phrases, or connect clauses. Clauses are sections of a sentence that hold at least one subject and a verb. For example, the sentence *Yo voy a ir a la playa porque quiero nada* (I am going to the beach because I want to swim) contains two clauses: a main clause which can stand on its own "*Yo voy a la playa,*" and one subordinate clause that can only make sense when paired with a main clause "porque quiero nadar." To join these clauses, words, or phrases, conjunctions are necessary to fit the role. There are different kinds of conjunctions that are utilized in varying situations. Spanish conjunctions, like English conjunctions, come in many forms and styles that have certain utility. This section will detail how to use and attach conjunctions to their corresponding place properly.

Common Spanish Conjunctions

The table below will feature the most common conjunctions used in Spanish, as well as accompanying examples:

Spanish Conjunction	Example Sentence
y (and)	*Yo tengo hambre y sueño.* (I am hungry and sleepy.)
o (or)	*A mi no me gusta la nieve o la lluvia.* (I don't like snow or rain).
pero (but)	*Iba a comer, pero me llamaron.* (I was going to eat, but they called me.)
porque (because)	*Me encanta el día porque está*

	soleado. (I love the day because it's sunny.)
sino (but/rather)	*Ella no vino a trabajar, sino a jugar.* (She didn't come to work, but to play.)
entonces (then)	*Entonces, ¿cúando nos vamos?* (Then, when are we leaving?)
ni (neither)	*Él no es alto ni calvo.* (He is neither tall or bald.)
mientras (as/while)	*Mientras comías, salí al parque.* (While you ate, I went to the park.)
dónde (where)	*Con permiso, ¿dónde encontramos?* (Excuse me, where are we?)
apenas (as soon as)	*Apenas la veá, la voy a abrazar.* (As soon as I see her, I'll hug her.)
Desde que (since)	*He tenido sed desde que salimos del hotel.* (I've been thirsty since we left the hotel).

With just these few conjunctions, any kind of phrase, expression, or question can be created. Conjunctions are necessary to clarify information and connect thoughts and ideas to one another. Of course, there is a bit more about conjunctions that need to be specified.

Varying Forms: Y & O

It's important to mention that two certain conjunctions have two varying forms: *y* (and) and *o* (or). When *y* comes before a word that begins with an *i–* or an *hi–*, the conjunction *y* changes into *e*. Furthermore, when *o* comes before a word that begins with an *o–* or an *ho–*, then the conjugation *o* changes into *u*. The table below will demonstrate these forms in some examples:

Spanish Conjunction	Example Sentence
e (and)	*Yo hablo frances e inglés.* (I speak French and English.)
	¿Dónde está Roberto e Isaac? (Where are Roberto and Isaac?)
	Necesito comprar bebidas e hielo. (I need to buy drinks and ice.)
u (or)	*¿Quíeres ir a Bilbao u Oviedo?* (Do you want to go to Bilbao or Oviedo?)
	Debo tomar el tren para Córdoba u Oriza. (I need to take the train to Cordoba or Oriza.)
	Di "buenas noches" u "hola" cuando la veas. (Say "goodnight" or "hello" when you see her.)

Conjunctions are essential to sounding native and eloquent in Spanish. By memorizing these few rules, any and all sentences will be elevated by the complexity of their thoughts.

1.8 Prepositions

Prepositions, similar to conjunctions, are connecting words. Prepositions connect nouns to other nouns or nouns to verbs to clarify the relationship between those words. Examples of prepositions include "about," "to," "near," "with," and "since." In the sentence, "The city map was below the pillow," "below" is the preposition that specifies the relationship between the noun "the city map" and the other noun "the pillow." Imagine that, in the mountains of Peru, a guide turns to his tourist group and says: "The pack of llamas ran through the hills near the lake." In this example, "of," "through," and "near" are all examples of prepositions that further explain the guide's message. The difference between prepositions and conjunctions is that prepositions specify placement and ownership. In Spanish, unlike English, prepositions maintain their form, but their definition changes, depending on their placement in a sentence.

Common Prepositions

The table below features some of the most commonly used prepositions, as well as sample sentences:

Spanish Preposition	Example Sentence
desde (from, since)	*Yo no la he visto desde ayer.* (I haven't seen her since yesterday.)
en (in, on, at)	*Perdí mi teléfono en el tren.* (I lost my phone on the train.)
a (to, at)	*Yo voy en camino a Costa Rica.* (I am on my way to Costa Rica).

hasta (until, toward)	*Yo no te veré hasta mañana.* (I won't see you until tomorrow.)
con (with)	*Yo fuí con mis amigos.* (I went with my friends.)
de (of, from)	*De la noche a la tarde, te extrañé.* (From night to day, I missed you.)
sin (without)	*Quiero un café sin leche.* (I want a coffee without milk.)

Generally, Spanish prepositions are used in the same way as English prepositions; that is, understanding their placement and usage will be reasonably easy to comprehend, especially when seeing the context of a sentence. Still, as previously mentioned, some Spanish prepositions require a bit of extra attention because they have many meanings.

Special Prepositions: A, De, & En

The preposition *a* is an extensively common preposition that has various definitions; the table below reviews the meanings of this one-letter preposition:

Spanish Preposition: a	
To indicate movement	*Iré al rio en domingo.* (I will go to the river on Sunday.)

To connect a verb to another verb	*Yo empecé a cocinar.* (I began to cook).
To clarify the way something is done	*Yo escribí el libro a mano.* (I wrote the book by hand.)
To introduce an individual	*Ayer, conocí a Cata.* (Yesterday, I met Cata.)
To express a time	*El vuelo es a las 5:15 de la mañana.* (The flight is at 5:15 in the morning.)

The preposition *de* is another common preposition that has various definitions; the table below reviews the meanings of this Spanish preposition:

Spanish Preposition: de	
To indicate possession	*Bogotá es la cápital de Colombia* (I will go to the river on Sunday.)
To clarify cause	*Yo estoy feliz de comer paella.* (I am happy from eating paella).
To indicate origin	*Él es de Chile.* (He is from Chile.)

To compare	*Sofía es la más alta de la familia.* (Sofia is the tallest in the family.)
To describe a noun with another noun	*Yo amo la sopa de mariscos.* (I love seafood soup.)

Lastly, the preposition *en* is another common preposition that has various definitions; the table below reviews the meanings of this Spanish preposition:

Spanish Preposition: en	
To clarify location	*El cargador está en mi mochila.* (The charger is in my back bag.)
To specify time	*Yo fuí a Ecuador en el otoño.* (I went to Ecuador in the fall).
To indicate the way something is done	*Ellos fueron a Barcelona en tren.* (They went to Barcelona by train.)
To accompany common expressions	*en serio* (seriously) *en vivo* (live, as in live tv)

Spanish prepositions will certainly add a necessary flare and additional information to sentences. Prepositions will become an important staple for any speaker, the more practice that goes into learning the many uses and meanings. The end of this section signifies the end of the grammar portion of this book.

Now, we move on to common Spanish expression.

Chapter 2 - Spanish Phrases I: Common Expressions

2.1 Greetings, Farewells, & Manners

Greetings, farewells, and showing courtesy are the universal way to introduce ourselves to friends, family, and strangers. Offering someone a "Hello!" or a sincere "Take care!" is very important because it lets others know that you're a welcoming, respectful person. Sharing a warm greeting is especially important in Spanish culture. Both Spanish and Latin American individuals are known for being very inviting and jovial to everyone they come across; if a Colombian hugs you or an Uruguayan invites you to *un asado* (a cook-out) the first time they meet you, don't be surprised. Stepping into the Spanish culture means that you're now open to being friendlier and kinder to those around you. Because of this cultural affability, greetings are an important portion of learning Spanish. Anywhere you go, whoever you meet, amiability will always open doors to new friendships and experiences.

The table below offers the most commonly used greetings; this list includes acknowledgments that can be used in many contexts, from meeting up with a friend to speaking to a waiter in a restaurant. After the table, there will be examples of scenarios that offer new vocabulary words to add you your arsenal.

Spanish Greetings
hola (hello)
buenos días (good morning)
buenas tardes (good evening)
buenas noches (goodnight)
¿cómo estás? (how are you?)

bien/muy bien (good/very good)
¿qué onda? (what's up?)
¿qué pasa? (how are things?)
mucho gusto (nice to meet you)
encantado (pleased to meet you)
¿qué pasó? (what happened?)
¿de dónde eres? (where are you from?)
¿dónde vas? (where are you going?)
¿cómo te llamas? (what's your name?)
¿aló? (hello, when answering a call)

Scenario #1 - Going Out to Dinner

Waiter: *¡Hola! Buenas tardes, ¿cómo está?*
(Hello! Good evening, how are you?)

Carlos: *Estoy bien, ¡gracias! Y usted?*
(I'm well, thank you! And you?)

Waiter: *Muy bien, ¿le puedo traer agua?*
(Very well, can I bring you water?)

Carlos: *Sí, por favor. ¿Podría tener una copa de vino rojo tambien?*
(Yes, please. Could I also have a glass of red wine?)

Waiter: *Por supuesto, ahorita la traigo. ¿Necesíta tiempo para ver el menu?*
(Of course, I'll bring it right away. Do you need time to look over the menu?)

Carlos: *Si, por favor. Eso si, quiero una ensalada de tomates.*

(Yes, please. I do want a tomato salad.)

Waiter: *Le pondre la orden. ¿Quiere algo más con el vino?*
(I'll put in the order. Do you want to pair something else with the wine.)

Carlos: *No, estoy bien por ahora. Gracias.*
(No, I'm good for now. Thank you.)

Waiter: *Bueno, ¡ya regreso!*
(Okay, I'll be back!)

After the meal.

Waiter: *¿Cómo estuvo la comida?*
(How was the food?)

Carlos: *Excelente, estuvo deliciosa. La carne estaba tan tierna, y las papas hornadas fueron tan crujientes. ¡Me encantó!*
(Delicious, it was delicious. The meat was so tender, and the baked potatoes were so crispy. I loved it!)

Waiter: *¡Que bueno! ¿Quiére un cafecíto, ó el menu de postres?*
(That's great! Would you like a coffee or the dessert menu?)

Carlos: *El café, por favor. Y, ¿podría traerme la cuenta tambien?*
(A coffee, please. And could you also bring me the check, please?)

Waiter: *Ya enseguida traeré ambos.*
(I'll bring both right away.)

Carlos: *¡Muchas gracias!*
(Thank you so much!)

The meal is paid.

Waiter: *Gracias, cuídese. ¡Que tenga buenas noches!*
(Thank you, take care. Have a good night!)

Carlos: *Igualmente, ¡buenas noches!*
(You too, have a good night!)

Scenario #2 - Running Into a Friend

Morgan: *¡Michael! ¿Cómo estás?*
(Michael! How are you?)

Michael: *¡Morgan! ¡Te extrañé mucho! Ví que fuistes a Panama el mes pasado. ¿Cómo te fue?*
(Morgan! I missed you so much! I saw that you went to Panama last month. How'd it go?)

Morgan: *Si, estuvo increíble. Conocí a tantas personas y las playas fueron tan hermosas. Comí demasiado y descansé un monton.*
(Yes, it was incredible. I met tons of people, and the beaches were so beautiful. I ate so much, and I got to rest a lot.)

Michael: *Me encanta. ¿Nós podemos reunir éste viernes?*
(That's awesome! Can we meet up this Friday?)

Morgan: *¡Bueno! Envíame un texto, por favor. Ahí averigüamos los detalles.*
(Okay! Send me a text, please. We'll figure out the details.)

Michael: *¡Okay! Cuidate, te quiero mucho. Y ten un buen día.*
(Okay! Take care; I love you. Have a great day.)

Morgan: *Ciao, ¡besitos!*
(Bye, kisses!)

Offering a Farewell

The following table offers the most commonly used phrases to say goodbye to someone; this list includes acknowledgments that can be used in many contexts, from speaking to a cash register at a supermarket to a taxi driver, to asking a stranger for directions. After the table, there will be examples of scenarios that offer new vocabulary words to add you your arsenal.

Farewell Remarks
adios/ciao (goodbye)
hasta luego (see you later)
hasta mañana (see you tomorrow)
cuídate (take care)
tenga un buen día (have a good day)

Scenario #1 - Going to the Supermarket

Cash Register: *¡Hola! Buenas días, ¿cómo está hoy?*
(Hello! Good morning, how are you today?)

Martha: *Muy bien, gracias. ¿Y tú?*
(Very well. And yourself?)

Cash Register: *Igualmente, el día está fresco y soliado. ¿Vas hacer algo este fin de semana?*
(Likewise, the day is cool and sunny. Are you gonna do something this weekend?)

Martha: *Si, el clima está fenomenal. Y voy a salir con unos amigos – va ser divertido.*
(Yes, the weather is phenomenal. And I'm going out with some friends — it'll be fun.)

Cash Register: *Que bueno. ¿Encontró hoy todo lo que buscaba?*

(That's good. Did you find everything you were looking for today?)

Martha: *Si, si pudé. Las manzanas y las uvas se miraban maravillosas.*
(Yes, yes I did. The apples and the grapes looked marvelous.)

Cash Register: *Las frutas y las verduras estan buenísimas durante esta temporada. Bien, su factura de hoy es de $28.73. ¿Pagará con efectivo o con tarjeta de crédito?*
(The fruits and vegetables are excellent during this season. Okay, your total for today is $28.73. Will you be paying with cash or credit card?)

Martha: *Con tarjeta de crédito.*
(With a credit card.)

Cash Register: *Muy bien. Puede pagar con en escáner.*
(Very good. You can pay with the scanner.)

The groceries are paid.

Martha: *Muchas gracias, que tenga un buen día. ¡Cuídate!*
(Thank you so much, have a great day. Take care!)

Cash Register: *Igual a usted, cuídese.*
(Same to you; take care.)

Scenario #2 - Taking a Taxi

Taxi Driver: *Hola señor, ¿cómo está?*
(Hello, sir. How are you?)

Paul: *Me siento excelente, ¿me puede llavar al aeropuerto Jorge Chávez?*
(I feel excellent. Could you drive me to Jorge Chávez airport?

Taxi Driver: *Por supuesto, ya ahorita. ¿Va a recoger a algien?*

(Of course, right away. Are you picking up someone?

Paul: *Sí, a mi mejor amigo que viene de Nueva York a visitarme. No lo he visto en unos años – ambos estamos emocionados.*
(Yes, my best friend who's coming from New York to visit me. I haven't seen him in a few years — we're both excited.)

Taxi Driver: *Suena muy divertido, y ¿por cuánto tiempo se quedará en Lima?*
(That sounds really fun. And for how long is he staying in Lima?)

Paul: *Solo por dos semanas, pero haremos un monton de viajes por Perú.*
(Just for two weeks, but we'll do tons of traveling through Peru.

Taxi Driver: *Deben, se la pasarán muy bien.*
(You must. You'll both have a great time.)

Arrived at the airport.

Taxi Driver: *Muy bien, serán 52 soles.*
(Very well. It'll be 52 Peruvian soles.)

Paul: *Aquí estan y cuédese con el vuelto.*
(Here they are, and keep the change.)

Taxi Driver: *Muy hamable, nos vemos otro día. Adios.*
(Much appreciated, see you on another day. Goodbye.)

Paul: *Que tenga una buena tarde. ¡Ciao!*
(Have a great afternoon. Goodbye!)

Scenario #3 - Asking For Directions

Luís: *Hola, perdon señora. ¿Sábe dónde puedo encontrar la estación de Palos de la Frontera?*

(Hello, pardon ma'am. Do you know where I can find the Palos de la Frontera station?)

Stranger: *Sí, lo que harás es caminar tres bloques por la Calle de Canarias, y despues girarás a la derecha cuando llegués al Paseo de las Delicias. La estación estará en la escuina, entre Delicias y Ancora.*
(Yes, what you'll do is walk three blocks on Canarias Street, and then you'll make a right turn when you get to the Delicias Passageway. The station will be in the corner, between Delicias and Ancora.

Luís: *Entonces, ¿no estoy tan lejos?*
(So, I'm not that far?)

Stranger: *No, estás cerquita.*
(No, you're really close).

Luís: *Que bien, ¡muchas gracias! ¡Que tenga un buen día.*
(That's great, thank you! Have a great day.)

Stranger: *No hay problema, y buena suerte.*
(No problem, and good luck.)

Luís: *¡Ciao! Gracias una vez más.*
(Goodbye! Thank you again.)

Courtesy and Manners

The following table offers the most commonly used phrases to demonstrate courtesy to others; this list includes acknowledgments that can be used in many different contexts, from speaking to personnel at a train station to speaking to a barista at a café and buying a movie ticket at the theater. After the table, there will be examples of scenarios that offer new vocabulary words to add you your arsenal.

Expressions of Courtesy
bienvenido (welcome)
gracias/muchas gracias (thank you/thank you very much)
de nada (you're welcome)
por favor (please)

Scenario #1 - Buying a Metrocard

Sandra: *Hola, buenas noches. Tengo una pregunta acerca de la variedad de tarjetas de metro.*
(Hello, good evening. I have a question regarding the variety of metrocards.)

Metro Personnel: *Bienvenida, ¿cómo la puedo ayudar?*
(Welcome, how could I help you?)

Sandra: *Si compro una tarjeta de metro para la semana entera, ¿cuándo comenzarán los fondos: el domingo o el lunes?*
(If I buy a metrocard for the entire week, when would the funds begin: Sunday or Monday?)

Metro Personnel: *Comenzarían el lunes a las cinco de la mañana.*
(They would start on Monday at five in the morning.)

Sandra: *A bueno, voy a comprar una entonces.*
(Oh, okay, I'll buy one then.)

Metro Personnel: *Muy bien, será $24.*
(Very good, it'll be $24).

Metrocard is paid.

Sandra: *Muchas gracias. Disfrute su fin de semana.*
(Thank you very much. Enjoy your weekend.)

Metro Personnel: *Igualmente. Adios.*
(Likewise. Goodbye.)

Scenario #2 - Ordering at a Café

Joshua: *Hola, ¿puedo tener un macchiato mediano, por favor?*
(Hello, could I have a medium macchiato, please?)

Barista: *Por supuesto. ¿Le gustaría que le deje espacio para la leche?*
(Of course. Would you like me to leave space for some milk?)

Joshua: *Si, gracias. Y dame un croissant de chocolate, por favor.*
(Yes, thank you. And give me a chocolate muffin, please.)

Barista: Ahora lo traigo. *¿Quíere que se lo caliente en el orno?*

Joshua: *Si, por favor. ¿Cómo cuanto se tarda para calentar el croissant?*
(Yes, please. About how long does it take to heat the croissant?

Barista: *Solo un par de segundos, señor. Entonces, el total de hoy es $6.50.*
(Just a few seconds, sir. So, today's total is $6.50.)

Joshua: *Aquí está.*
(Here you go.)

Pays for order.

Barista: *Excelente, aquí está su cambio. Puede esperar en un mesa y le traeremos el café y el pastel.*
(Excellent. Here's your change. You can wait at a table, and we'll bring you the coffee and pastry.)

Joshua: *Muchísimas gracias, que tenga un buen día.*
(Thank you lots, have a great day.)

Barista: *Ni un problema. Que disfruté la comida.*
(No problem at all. Enjoy your food.)

Scenario #3 - Buying a Movie Ticket

Theater Cashier: *Hola, bienvenidos. ¿Cómo los puedo ayudar?*
(Hello, welcome. How could I help the both of you?)

Rachael: *Hola, ¿podemos tener dos entradas para "The Blue Times" a las 3:15?*
(Hello, could we have two tickets for "The Blue Times" for the 3:15 showing?)

Theater Cashier: *Si, por supuesto. Por favor escojan sus asientos en la pantalla.*
(Yes, of course. Please choose both your seats on the screen.)

Rachael: *Bueno.*
(Okay.)

Theater Cashier: *Ambos boletos serán $22. ¿Tiénen una miembresía para el cine?*
(Both tickets will be $22. Do either of you have a movie theater membership?)

Rachael: *No, pero estamos bien, gracias. Aquí está mi tarjeta de debito.*
(No, but we are fine, thanks. Here is my debit card.)

Theater Cashier: *Bueno, muchas gracias. Y aquí está su recibo. ¡Que disfruten la pelicula!*

(Okay, thank you very much. And here's your receipt. Enjoy the movie!)

Rachael: *Lo haremos, buenas noches.*

(We will. Have a good night.)

2.2 Colors

Colors are an important quality in the world. Everything features distinct shades of pinks and blues, whites, and oranges. From clothing to food, vehicles, books, and houses — everything around us embodies color and texture. In this section, the Spanish names for colors will be explored in a variety of scenarios. As it was explored in the previous chapter, most colors have both a masculine and feminine form, as well as a singular and plural form. However, some colors do not have a feminine form, and thus, those specific colors are expressed and written only in their masculine form. The table below features various colors throughout the spectrum; the example scenarios will illustrate how to mention these colors in their corresponding forms.

Color in Spanish
rojo (red)
naranja (orange)
amarillo (yellow)
verde (green)
azul (blue)
morado (purple)
rosado (pink)

maron (brown)
negro (black)
blanco (white)
gris (grey)

Scenario 1 - Buying New Pants

Chris: *Brit, ¿cuáles te gustan más: los pantalones azules o los grises?*
(Brit, which pair do you prefer: the blue pants or the grey ones?)

Britt: *Honestamente, ninguno me gustan. Los azules son muy grandes y los grises se ven bien cortos de las piernas.*
(Honestly, I don't like either. The blue ones are too big, and the grey ones look too short at the legs.)

Chris: *¿Qué hago entonces? A mi no me gustaron los otros pares en esta tienda.*
(What should I do then? I didn't like the other pairs in this store.)

Britt: *¿Y estos rojos? ¿No te gustan?*
(And these red ones? Do you like them?)

Chris: *Sí son bonitos, me los voy a medir. A ver si me quedan bien.*
(Yes they're nice, I'll try them on. Let's see if they'll fit me well.)

Britt: *Bueno, me quedo sentada aquí esperandote.*
(Okay, I'll stay seated here waiting for you.)

Returns from the fitting room.

Chris: *¿Cómo se ven? En realidad, al principio el color no me convencío, pero es un rojo brillante y bonito. Y dan con todo.*

(How do they look? In reality, the color didn't convince me at first, but it's a brilliant, nice red. And they match with everything.)

Britt: *¡Me encantan! Te ves tan bien. Sí, dan con la mayoriía de camisetas que tienes en el ropero en la casa.*

(I love them! You look so great. Yes, they match most of the shirts you have in your wardrobe at home.)

Chris: *Creó que los voy a comprar. Wow, mira, están en descuento – 50% menos que el precio original.*

(I think I'll take them. Wow, look, they're discounted 50% off the original price.)

Britt: *¡Tienes que comprarlos! Son una buena oferta.*
(You have to buy them! They're such a good offer.)

Chris: *Si, tienes razón. Vamos para pagar por ellos.*
(Yes, you're right. Let's go pay for them.)

Britt: *¡Si! ¡Vamos!*
(Yes! Let's go!)

Scenario #2 - Renting a Car

Mark: *Hola, buenas tardes. Me gustaría alquilar un auto por tres días. Hando buscando un model de este año. Puede ser de cualquier marca de carros.*

(Hello, good afternoon. I would like to rent a car for three days. I'm looking for a model from this year. It can be from whichever car brand.)

Empleada: *Encantada de ayudarlo, señor. Ahorita mismo, tenemos cuatro modelos diferentes que coíncidan con la description que me está dando.*

(Pleasure to help you, sir. Right now, we have four different models that match the description that you're giving me.)

Mark: *Maravilloso, ¿y cuánto pagaría por rentar un auto por tres días?*
(Wonderful. And how much would it be to rent a car for three days?)

Empleada: *El total sería...$150. ¿Suena bien?*
(The total would be...$150. Sounds good?)

Mark: *Suéna fantastico, acepto la oferta entonces.*
(It sounds fantastic; I accept the offer.)

Empleada: *Muy bien, ¿y cuál de las cuatro modelos de gustaría elegir? Son de la misma marca y tienen el mismo estilo. Tenemos uno negro, uno gris, un verde y un carro blanco.*
(Very good, and which of the four models would you like to choose? They're from the same brand and have similar styles. We have a black one, a grey one, a green one, and a white car.)

Mark: *Me encanta el negro – se ve muy elegante. Pero el verde es mi color favorito, así que me voy a llevar en auto verde.*
(I love the black one; it looks very elegant. But green is my favorite color, so I'll take the green car.)

Empleada: *Excelente, el verde es un color muy bonito. Firme aquí, y le traigo las llaves del auto.*
(Excellent, green is a very pretty color. Sign here, and I'll bring you the car keys.)

Mark: *Muchas gracias, señorita.*
(Thank you so much, ma'am.)

Empleada: *¡Claro! Aquí están las llaves del carro. Que disfrute el auto y que tenga un buen día.*
(Of course! Here are the car keys. Enjoy the car and have a great day.)

Mark: *Mil gracias, e igualmete.*
(A thousand thank-you's, and you too.)

Empleada: *Sin problema, iadios!*
(Anytime, goodbye!)

2.3 Orders, Numerals, & Numbers

Numbers are quintessential tools in our everyday lives. Numbers quantify and bring order to objects, placements, and people. Whether someone's competing for the first place or your spouse asks a mechanic to change three tires, numbers enable us all to share and explain important information. Just as in English, numbers have a massive place in Spanish. In this section, we'll explore how to utilize numbers in Spanish in various contexts. It's important to note that, in Spain and Latin American countries, some numbers are written differently than they would be in the US. For example, prices in Spain and Latin America are written as "$6,00" instead of "6.00," which means "1,000" becomes "1.000." But this section will facilitate the different uses, expressions, and forms of numbers.

Numbers in Spanish

The table below will depict the numbers 0-1000; it's important to take notice of how the written form changes after number 30.

Numeral	Cardial	Numeral	Cardial
0	cero	26	veintiseis
1	uno	27	veintisiete
2	dos	28	veintiocho
3	tres	29	veintinueve
4	cuatro	30	treinta
5	cinco	31	treinta y uno
6	seis	32	treinta y dos

7	*siete*	33	*treinta y tres*
8	*ocho*	34	*treinta y cuatro*
9	*nueve*	35	*treinta y cinco*
10	*diez*	36	*treinta y seis*
11	*once*	37	*treinta y siete*
12	*doce*	38	*treinta y ocho*
13	*trece*	39	*treinta y nueve*
14	*catorce*	40	*cuarenta*
15	*quince*	50	*cincuenta*
16	*dieciséis*	60	*sesenta*
17	*diecisiete*	70	*setenta*
18	*dieciocho*	80	*ochenta*
19	*diecinueve*	90	*noventa*
20	*veinte*	100	*cien*
21	*veiniuno*	200	*doscientos*
22	*veintidós*	300	*trescientos*
23	*veintitres*	400	*cuatrocientos*
24	*veinticuatro*	500	*quinientos*
25	*veinticinco*	1000	*mil*

The following table will demonstrate the numeral ordinal forms necessary to create lists and placements in both masculine and feminine forms:

Numeral	Ordinal
1	primero/primera
2	segundo/segunda
3	tercero/tercera
4	quarto/quarta
5	quinto/quinta
6	sexto/sexta
7	séptimo/séptima
8	octavo/octava
9	noveno/novena
10	décimo/décima

The following example scenarios will illustrate the many ways numbers can be used in Spanish.

Scenario #1 - Making a List

Julio: *¿Qué tenemos que hacer hoy?*
(What do we have to do today?)

David: *Primero, tenemos que llevar al perro a pasear. Segundo, tenemos que comprar comida para la semana. Tercero, llamar a la compañía de eléctricida. Y cuarto, debémos limpiar la sala.*
(First, we need to walk the dog. Second, we need to buy groceries for the week. Third, call the electric company. And fourth, we should clean the living room.)

Julio: *Yo puedo llevar al pero y tú puedes ir y comprar la comida. Luego, volvemos y limpiamos la sala juntos.*
(I can take the dog out, and you can go and buy the groceries. Then, we can come back and clean the living room together.)

David: *Suena bien. Y, ¿quién llamará a la compañía eléctrica?*
(Sounds good. And who's gonna call the electric company?)

Julio: *Esta será la tercera vez que llamamos a ese lugar y todavía no solucionan el problema.*
(This will be the third time we call that place, and they haven't solved the problem.)

David: *Esperemos que esta vez sea la última.*
(Hopefully, this time is the last.)

Julio: *Bueno, ahí nos vemos despues.*
(Okay, see you later.)

David: *Adios amigo.*
(Bye, dude.)

Scenario #2 - Ordering Multiples

Jenny: *¡Hola! Quiero comprar una docena de macarons.*
(Hello. I want to buy a dozen macarons.)

Pastelera: *Sí claro, ¿qué sabores quieres? Tenemos varios disponibles.*
(Yes, of course, which flavors would you like? We have many available.)

Jenny: *Quiero tres de café, tres de vainilla, dos de chocolate, uno de pistacho y – ¿qué sabor es el morado?*
(I want three coffee ones, three vanilla ones, two chocolate ones, one pistachio, and — what flavor is the purple one?)

Pastelera: *El morado es de arándano.*

(The purple one is blueberry.)

Jenny: *¡Que rico! Dame tres de esos, por favor.*
　　　(Yummy! Give me three of those, please.)

Pastelera: *Ahorita mismo.*
　　　(Right away.)

Jenny: *¡Gracias!*
　　　(Thank you!)

2.4 Times & Dates

Times and dates are a continuation of the previous section. As previously proven, numbers have infinite utilities and forms. In this section, we'll explore how to speak about times during the day, as well as dates of the year. It's important to note that, because Spain and Latin American countries use the metric system, unlike the US that uses the imperial system, times and dates are expressed differently in Hispanic nations. For example, 6:00 PM in the US would be written as 18:00 in Spain. These differences will be further explored and simplified in the tables and example scenarios below.

Times of Day

Similar to English, Spanish time is expressed with the verb *ser* (is). For example, "It's six twenty-five," becomes *Son las seis y veinticinco*. The table below illustrates the general form to express time in Spanish:

One O'Clock	*From Two to Twelve O'Clock*
es la una y ____	*son las ____ y ____*
(It's one ____)	(It's ____ ____)

A few examples include *es la una y cino* (it's one o'five), *es la una y cuarenta y cinco* (it's one forty-five), *son las siete y veinte* (it's seven twenty), *son las once y diez* (it's eleven ten).

To specify it's half-past the hour, in Spanish, it would be ____ *y media* (it's ____ thirty), as in, *son las cinco y media* (it's five thirty).

To express that it's a quarter past the hour, in Spanish, it woud be ____ *y cuarto* (it's ____ fifteen), as in, *son las dos y cuarto* (it's two fifteen).

The table below includes some important Spanish phrases that detail specific times during the day:

Temporal Spanish Phrases
de la mañana   (in the morning)
de la tarde   (in the afternoon)
De la noche   (at night)
en punto   (on the dot)
más o menos   (around, roughly)
medianoche   (midnight)

mediodía
(midday)
tempranísimo
(very early)
tardísimo
(very late)

Dates in Spanish

The table below will show the months of the year in Spanish, as well as provide examples on how to properly state dates. Note that in Spanish, the day comes before the month and year:

Month	Example Phrase
enero (January)	el ocho de enero (January 8)
febrero (February)	el diez de febrero (February 10)
marzo (March)	el veinticuatro de marzo (March 24)
abril (April)	el primero de abril (April 1st)
mayo (May)	el siete de mayo (May 7)

junio (June)	*el doce de junio* (June 12)
julio (July)	*el treinta y uno de julio* (July 31)
agosto (August)	*el diecinueve de agosto* (August 19)
septiembre *(September)*	*el cinco de septiembre* (September 5)
octubre *(October)*	*el catorse de octubre* (October 14)
noviembre (November)	*el veintiocho de noviembre* (November 28)
dicienbre (December)	*el veinticinco de diciembre* (December 25)

It's evident in the table above that the format to mention date is as follows:

> *el ____ de ____ del ____*

For example, *el ocho de abril del dos mil diecinueve* (April 8, 2019). In regular metrical form, the date would be written as (08/04/19).

The following example scenarios will illustrate the many ways to express time and dates in Spanish.

Scenario #1 - Asking for the Date

Ruben: *Permiso chico, ¿cuál es la fecha de hoy?*
    (Excuse me, young man, what's today's date?)

Stranger: *Es el cuatro de febrero del dos mil dieciocho.*
    (It's February 4, 2018.)

Ruben: *¡Muchas gracias!*
    (Thank you so much!)

Stranger: *Ni un problema.*
    (No problem.)

Scenario #2 - Scheduling a Time

Luz: *¿Quieres cenar en un restaurante?*
    (Do you want to get dinner at a restaurant?)

Edwin: *Sí, me encantaría. ¿Podemos ir a un lugar mexicano?*
    (Yes, I'd love to. Can we go to a Mexican place?)

Luz: *¡Okay! Suena bien.*
    (Okay! Sounds good.)

Edwin: *¿Nos juntamos a las siete y media de la noche?*
    (Want to get together at 7:30 PM?)

Luz: *Sí, a esa hora salgo del trabajo.*
    (Yes, I get out of work at that time.)

Edwin: *Suena perfecto. ¡Te miro en un rato!*
    (Sounds perfect. I'll see you in a bit!)

Luz: *¡Te miro! Ciao.*
    (See ya! Goodbye.)

2.5 Family & Friends

Family and friends entail some of our most important interdependent relationships. We rely on both family members and friends to navigate life, overcome obstacles, and gain more understanding about ourselves through them. In Spanish culture, family and friends are the nuclei of the society; there is nothing more important in the world than spending time with loved ones, creating memories for decades. Because of this, Spaniards and Latin Americans are known for being collectivistic people. That is, extended family, neighbors, and acquaintances are all as important as immediate family members, like parents and siblings. The sense of community is one that's pivotal for Spanish culture, and in this section, we'll explore the many figures that family units are comprised of.

Family Members and Friends

The table below will illustrate the different ways to denote family members and confidants. Following the table, an example scenario will be shown to illustrate further the usage of the Spanish terms:

Spanish Terms
mamá
(mom)
papá
(dad)
hermano/hermana
(brother/sister)
abuelo/abuela
(grandfather/grandmother)
tio/tia

(uncle/aunt)
primo/prima
(cousin/cousin (feminine))
vecino/vecina
(neighbor/neighbor (feminine))
amigo/amiga
(friend/friend (feminine))
mejor amigo/mejor amiga
(best friend/best friend (feminine))

Scenario #1 - Calling Mom

Robert: *¿Aló, mamá? ¿Cómo estás?*
(Hello, mom? How are you?)

Mom: *¡Hola, hijo! Estoy bien, aquí almorzando con tu abuela. Y tú, ¿cómo está todo en Los Ángeles?*
(Hello, son! I'm good; I'm having lunch with your grandmother. And you, how's everything in Los Angeles?)

Robert: *¡Todo está bien! Finalice el contrato de mi departamento y le cambié la matrícula al auto. Asi que oficialmente soy un residente de California.*
(Everything's going well! I finalized my apartment's lease, and I changed my car's registration. So I'm officially a resident of California.)

Mom: *Que bien, hijo. Me alegro por tí. ¿Has hablado con tu papá para contarle las buenas nuevas?*

(That's great, son. I'm happy for you. Have you spoken to your dad to tell him the good news?)

Robert: *Aún no. Solo pude llamarte a ti y a Richard.*
(Not yet. I only got the chance to call you and Richard.)

Mom: *Bien, y ¿cómo está tu hermano?*
(Good, and how is your brother?)

Robert: *Me contó que todo está bien. Le ofrecieron un ascenso en el trabajo y me dijo que la va ha aceptar.*
(He told me everything's going well. They offered him a promotion at his job and that he's going to accept it.)

Mom: *¡Maravilloso! ¿Has oído de Sharon?*
(Marvellous! Have you heard from Sharon?)

Robert: *Hablé con ella la semana pasada. Me conto que se siente estresada por sus exámenes finales, pero que también está bien.*
(I spoke to her last week. She told me that she's feeling stressed over her final exams, but that she's also fine.)

Mom: *Me alegra mucho que tu hermanita este bien. Bueno, Robert, te voy a dejar para regresar al almuerzo con tu abuelita. ¡Te manda saludos!*
(That makes me so happy that your little sister is doing well. Okay, Robert, I'll let you go and go back to lunch with your grandma. She sends you blessings!)

Robert: *De acuerdo, mamá. Te quiero mucho y saludas a mi abuela por mí. Y que disfruten su almuerzo juntas*
(Okay, mom. I love you and say hi to grandma for me. Hope you enjoy your lunch together.)

Mom: *Lo haré, hijo. Yo también te quiero mucho. ¡Adios!*
(I will, son. I love you too. Bye!)

Robert: *Adios, mami.*
(Bye, mom.)

Mom: *Okay, ¡ciao!*
   (Okay, bye!)

2.6 Feelings & Emotional States

Emotions are an important part of human psychology. They dictate how someone feels, how they act, how they carry themselves, and how they perceive the world. It's essential to express one's emotional states to those in proximity — not to come off as rude or glum. If someone's feeling happy, they want to share that with a friend. If they're feeling sad or stressed out, it's important to have someone by their side to comfort one another. In this section, we will explore the various Spanish terms for emotional states, as well as provide example scenarios to illustrate the terms' usage.

Emotions Galore

The table below will clarify the different terms to denote certain *emociones* (emotions) and *sentimientos* (feelings). Following the table, two example scenarios will be shown to further illustrate the usage of the Spanish terms:

Emotions and Feelings
feliz   (happy)
triste   (sad)
enojado/enojada   (angry/angry (feminine))
emocionado/emocionada   (excited/excited (feminine))

asustado/asustada
(scared/scared (feminine))
celoso/celosa
(jealous/jealous (feminine))
nervioso/nerviosa
(nervous/nervous (feminine))
preocupado/preocupada
(worried/worried (feminine))
furioso/furiosa
(furious/furious (feminine))
avergonzado/avergonzada
(embarrased/embarrased (feminine))
cansado/cansada
(tired/tired (feminine))
aburrido/aburrida
(bored/bored (feminine))
confundido/confundida
(confused/confused (feminine))
relajado/relajada
(relaxed/relaxed (feminine))
perdido/perdida
(lost/lost (feminine))

To express emotional states in Spanish, the emotion or feeling would be paired up with *me siento* (I feel) and *estoy* (I am). For example, *me siento fatal* (I feel terrible) and *estoy fabulosa* (I am fabulous).

Scenario #1 - Speaking to a Friend

Alex: *Hola, Paulo. ¿Cómo estás?*
(Hey, Paulo. How are you?)

Paulo: *Pues, me siento un poco triste.*
(Well, I feel a bit sad).

Alex: *¿Por qué? ¿Pasó algo?*
(Why? Did something happen?)

Paulo: *Mi cachorro, Sol, se sentía enfermo y lo tuve que llevar al veterinario. Él todavía está hospitalizado.*
(My puppy, Sol, was feeling ill, and I had to take him to the veterinarian. He's still hospitalized.)

Alex: *¡Que terrible! Lo siento mucho. ¿Qué le pasa al perrito?*
(That's terrible! I'm so sorry. What's wrong with the puppy?"

Paulo: *Los médicos creen que Sol se comió un pedazo de chocolate accidentalmente. Lo están monitoriando para asegurarse que se vaya a mejorar sin complicaciones a su sistema digestivo.*
(The doctors believe that Sol accidentally ate a piece of chocolate. They're monitoring him to make sure he'll get better without complications to his digestive system.)

Alex: *Espero que todo salga bien con Sol. Por favor, avísame cuando tengas más noticias.*
(I hope that everything goes well with Sol. Please, let me know when you have new updates.)

Paulo: *Lo haré. Gracias por preocuparte por Sol.*
(I will. Thank you for worrying about Sol).

Alex: *¡Claro! Hablamos más tarde entonces. Cuídate, Paulo.*
(Of course! We'll talk later then. Take care, Paulo.)

Paulo: *Tú también, Alex.*
(You too, Alex.)

Scenario #2 - Small Talk

Amy: *¡Alicia! Te ves tan linda, ¿cómo estás?*
(Alicia! You look so pretty; how are you?)

Alicia: *¡Estoy bien emocionada! Voy a una cita ahora mismo.*
(I'm very excited! I'm going on a date right now.)

Amy: *Qué divertido. ¿Van a un restaurante?*
(How fun. Are you going to a restaurant?)

Alicia: *Sí, vamos a conseguír comida italiana. Despues iremos al parque al lado del río para caminar un poco.*
(Yes, we're going to get Italian food. Then we'll go to the park next to the river to walk for a bit.)

Amy: *Hermoso, ¡que se disfruten!*
(Beautiful, hope you both enjoy it!)

Alicia: *¡Gracias! Cuídate, Amy. Adios.*
(Thank you! Take care, Amy. Bye.)

Amy: *¡Tú tambien! Ciao.*
(You too! Bye.)

2.7 Health

Health is yet another important aspect of everyday living. One's moods and energy levels are greatly impacted by how their body feels; if someone comes down with a cold, they probably feel lethargic and stuffy. If someone suffers from spring allergies, their skin might seem irritated and red. It's important to be able to express one's health status to others; in case of an emergency, everyone can be prepared and ready to go. In this section, we will explore the various Spanish terms for health-related topics, as well as provide example scenarios to clarify the terms' usage.

Symptoms and Illnesses

The tables below will illustrate the different terms to denote various adjectives, symptoms, illnesses, health-related facilities, and useful phrases in Spanish. Following the graphics, two example scenarios will be shown to further illustrate the usage of the Spanish terms:

Spanish Adjectives
irritado/irritada   (irritated/irritated (feminine))
dolorido/dolorida   (sore/sore (feminine))
inflamado/inflamada   (swollen/swollen (feminine))
sensible   (sensitive)

Symptoms in Spanish
migraña   (migraine)
vómito   (vomit)

tos
(coughing)
fiebre
(fever)
la nariz tapada
(stuffy nose)
dificultad para respirar
(difficulty breathing)
dolor
(pain)
un calabre
(a cramp)
mareo
(dizziness)
falta de balance
(imbalance)

Illnesses in Spanish
una alergia
(an allergy)
un resfrío
(a cold)
una herida
(an injury)
una fractura
(a fracture)
la gripe
(the flu)
diabetes
(diabetes)
artritis
(arthritis)
una quemadura
(a burn)
dolor de cabeza
(headache)

Health-Related Facilities in Spanish
el hospital   (the hospital)
la farmacia   (the pharmacy)
la sala de emergencias   (the emergency room)
la ambulancia   (the ambulance)

Useful Phrases in Spanish
estoy enfermo/enferma   (I am sick/sick (feminine))
no me siento bien   (I don't feel well)
tuve un accidente   (I had an accident)
¿dónde está el hospital?   (where is the hospital?)
necesito ayuda   (I need help)

me duele mi ____
(my ____ hurts)
¡llame a una ambulancia!
(call an ambulance!)

Scenario #1 - Needing Some Medication

Marta: *Josefa, ¿te sientes bien? Te ves un poco débil.*
(Josefa, are you feeling well? You look a bit weak.)

Josefa: *No, sinceramente, me duele la cabeza. No me puedo concentrar en mi trabajo.*
(No, honestly, my head hurts. I can't concentrate on my work.)

Marta: *¿Quieres que te tráiga un poco de agua? También tengo pastillas de ibuprofeno por si necesitas una.*
(Do you want me to bring you some water? I also have ibuprofen pills in case you need one.)

Josefa: *Sí, regálame una pastilla, por favor. Y tambien tráeme el agua para beberla. Gracias, Marta.*
(Yes, please, give me a pill. And bring me some water to drink it. Thank you, Marta.)

Marta: *Ni un problema, ya regreso.*
(No proplem, I'll be right back).

Returned with ibuprofen and water.

Marta: *Aquí está todo. Si necesitas otra pildora o más agua, avísame por favor.*
(Here's everything. If you need another pill or more water, please let me know.)

Josefa: *Muchas gracias, Marta. Te debo una.*
(Thank you so much, Marta. I owe you one.)

Marta: *Ni te preocupes. Todo estará bien, ya lo verás.*
(Don't even worry. Everything will be fine; you'll see.)

Scenario #2 - Helping a Stranger

Edward: *¡Ayuda! ¡Ayudenme!*
(Help! Someone help me!)

Someone ran over.

Stranger: *¿Qué pasó?*
(What happened?)

Edward: *Me caí de mi bicicleta, y creo que me fracture la pierna. ¡Me duele mucho!*
(I fell from my bicycle, and I think I fractured my leg. It hurts so much!)

Stranger: *¡Okay! Estoy llamando una ambulancia. ¡No te muevas!*
(Okay! I'm calling an ambulance. Don't move!)

Edward: *Intentaré de no moverla – ¡muchas gracias, señor!*
(I'll try not to move it. Thank you so much, sir!)

Chapter 3 - Spanish Phrases II: Standard Conversations

3.1 Questions & Answers

Often, everyday interactions involve both asking questions and responding to others' inquiries. Communication is generally a two-way street — one where the speaker sends a message to the receiver, the message is processed, and the receiver herself becomes the speaker, the speaker becomes the receiver, and so on. As explored in the previous chapter, dialogue can be short and simple. Or it can be extensive and complex. In this section, we'll expand on the common Spanish phrases introduced in the previous chapter. The example scenarios in this section have two main objectives: to provide new vocabulary and to sharpen conversational skills in Spanish.

At times, the characters in these example scenarios will send out confusing information to their receivers and will be forced to explain themselves further. As it's universally known, communication is not always seamless and perfect. Messages get tangled, some noise gets in the way, or even conflict rises when information is misunderstood. Pay close attention to how varied and dynamic the Spanish language can be.

Scenario #1 - Ordering a Cake

James: *¿Aló? Buenos días, ¿con quien hablo?*
    (Hello? Good morning, to who am I talking to?)

Baker: *Buenos días, señor. Habla con el dueño de la pastelería. ¿Cómo le podemos ayudar el día de hoy?*
    (Good morning, sir. You're speaking to the owner of the bakery. How can we help you today?)

James: *Muy bien, cuiciera saber si ustedes venden pasteles veganos?*
    (Very well, I'd like to know you if you guys sell vegan cakes?)

Baker: *Sí, sí vendemos pasteles veganos. Tenemos pasteles ya hechos y también podemos hacer pasteles a medida. Podemos hacerlos de una variedad de sabores y rellenos, incluyendo de frutas y de crema.*

(Yes, yes we sell vegan cakes. We have cakes already made, and we can also bake custom-made cakes. We can make them in a variety of flavors and fillings, including fruits and cremes.)

James: *Fantástico. Pero necesito el pastel para mañana – no sé si esto sería un problema para usted. Es para mi esposa que está cumpliendo años y quiero conseguírle un pastel especial.*

(Fantastic. But I need the cake for tomorrow — I don't know if this is a problem for you. It's for my wife's birthday, and I want to get her a special cake.)

Baker: *¿Para mañana? Lo siento, pero eso no nos daría suficiente tiempo para creár el pastel. Necesitamos por lo menos dos días para hacer un pastel vegano correctamente. Lo sentimos.*

(For tomorrow? I'm sorry, but that doesn't give us sufficient time to create the cake. We need at least two days to bake a vegan cake properly. We apologize.)

James: *¿En serió? ¿Y si pido un pastel vegano pequeño? Si no es tan grande, ¿lo prodrían hacer?*

(Seriously? And what if I ask for a small vegan cake? If it's not that big, could you guys make it?)

Baker: *Desafortunadamente, no podríamos hacer lo en un solo día. Si está interesado, siempre tenemos pasteles veganos ya hechos.*

(Unfortunately, we cannot make it in just one day. If you're interested, we still have vegan cakes already made.)

James: *Esos pasteles ya hechos no me llaman la atención. Mi esposa merece algo mejor, algo más único. ¿De verdad no me pueden hacer el pedido?*

(Those ready-made caked don't grab my attention. My wife deserves something better, something more unique. You really can't take my order?)

Baker: *Lastimosamente, no podemos ayudarlo. Si hubiera llamado ayer, esa ya sería otra historia. Pero hoy no se puede.*
(Sadly, we can't help you. If you would've called yesterday, that would've been a different story. But today, we cannot.)

James: *Que barbaridad. ¿Qué hago ahora? Yo pensé que iba recivir un servicio superior en comparación con otras patelerías de la ciudad.*
(That's awful. What do I do now? I thought I would receive superior service compared to other bakeries in the city.)

Baker: *Lo sentimos mucho por la inconveniencia.*
(We apologize greatly for the inconvenience.)

James: *Buscaré otra pastelería entonces. Una que sí me trate bien como el cliente.*
(Then I'll look for another bakery. One that will treat me well as the customer.)

Baker: *Buena suerte, señor. Que puéda encontrar lo que busca.*
(Good luck, sir. I hope you find what you are looking for.)

James: *Adios.*
(Goodbye.)

Baker: *Gracias por llamar. Adios.*
(Thank you for calling. Goodbye.)

Scenario #2 - Call With Bad Quality

April: *¿Aló? Scott, ¿le enviaste el informe financiero a Jackson?*
(Hello? Scott, did you send the financial report to Jackson?)

Scott: *¿Aló? ¿April? ¿Puédes repetir eso otra vez que no pude escucharte?*

(Hello? April? Can you say that again; I couldn't hear you?)

April: *Disculpá, es que hay una area de construcción cerca de mi parada de tren. Te pregunté si pudiste enviar el informe financiero a Jackson.*

(Sorry, there's a construction site near my train station. I asked you if you were able to send the financial report to Jackson.)

Scott: *Sí puedes escucharme, no puedo entender lo que me dices. Demasiado ruído.*

(If you can hear me, I can't understand what you're saying. Too much noise.)

April: *Voy a colgar y te voy a enviar un mensaje de texto. ¡Adios!*

(I'm going to hang up and send you a text message. Bye!)

Scott: *¿Aló? ¿April? Me colgó – que mal.*
(Hello? April? She hung up on me — bummer.)

3.2 General Description

Physical descriptions have a myriad of uses. Descriptions are necessary to identify a person, to set up an online work profile, to illustrate a car to a friend, or even to customize a dress. Descriptions are another quintessential part of speech, and in this section, we'll build upon adjectives and descriptors explores in previous sections. The example scenarios in this section will offer new adjectives and descriptive language that's important to note and practice.

Scenario #1 - Discussing a Date

Rose: *¿Cómo te fue tú cita de ayer?*
(How was your date yesterday?)

Sophie: *¡Estuvo maravillosa! Tom fue tan amable y tan, pero tan respetuoso. Me invitó a cenar, despues fuimos a ver una* *película y al final nos fuimos a su apartamento para platica. Me encantó.*

(It was marvelous! Tom was so nice and so, so respectful. He invited me to dinner, then we went to watch a movie, and lastly, we went to his apartment to chat. I loved it.)

Rose: *¡Que increíble! Me alegra tanto que se hayan divertido. Dime, ¿cómo se ve Tom? ¿Es alto, bajo, flaco, relleno? Quiero saber.*

(That's incredible! I'm so glad that you both had fun. Tell me, how does Tom look? Is he tall, short, thin, or chunky? I want to know.)

Sophie: *Él es alto, con pelo riso y ojos de miel. Tiene veintiocho años y vive en el centro de la ciudad. No es flaco ni relleno – tiene un cuerpo regular. Eso sí, le fascina correr, nadar e ir al gimnacio.*

(He's tall, with blond hair and eyes the color of honey. He's 28 years old, and he lives in the city's downtown area. He's not thin or chunky — he has an average body. Still, he enjoys running, swimming, and going to the gym.)

Rose: *Suena como un deseo hecho realidad. ¿Tendrá un amigo para mi? ¡Ja-ja-ja!*

(He sounds like a dream come true. Does he have a friend for me? Ha-ha-ha!)

Sophie: *¡Ja-ja-ja! ¡Juegas demasiado! Pero sí, hasta el momento me gusta pasar tiempo con el. Vamos a salir otra ves este fin de semana.*

(Ha-ha-ha! You play too much! But yes, until now I like spending time with him. We're going out again this weekend.)

Rose: *¿Dónde están planeando ir?*
(Where are you planning to go?

Sophie: *Le dije que fueramos al restaurante griego que queda por mi casa. Le conte que las ensaladas son exquicitas y la carne asada es tan jugosa. Dijo que iríamos ahí.*

(I told him that we should go to the Greek restaurant near my house. I let him know that the salads are exquisite and that the grilled meats are very juicy. He said we'll go there.)

Rose: *¡Se disfrutarán tanto! Por favor, déjame saber cómo les fue después de la cita.*
(You'll both enjoy it very much! Please, let me know how it went after the date.)

Sophie: *Por supuesto que te voy a contar todo. Ni te preocupes.*
(Of course, I'll tell you everything. Don't worry.)

Rose: *¡Gracias, amigua! Voy a comprar otro café, ¿quieres uno?*
(Thank you, bestie! I'm going to buy another coffee; do you want one?)

Sophie: *Sí, por favor. ¡Gracias!*
(Yes, please. Thank you!)

Rose: *Bueno, ¡ya vuelvo!*
(Okay, I'll be right back!)

Scenario #2 - Buying Some Shoes

Andrew: *Papá, no encuento un par de tenis que me guste. ¿Podemos ir a otra tienda?*
(Dad, I can't find a pair of sneakers that I like. Can we go to another store?)

Dad: *¿Y qué estilo estás buscando?*
(And what style are you looking for?

Andrew: *Quiero unos tenis blancos, que sean livianos y que me lleguen a los tobillos. Pero la mayoría de los zapatos aquí son botas pesadas.*
(I want white sneakers that are lightweight and rise up to my ankles. But the majority of shoes here are heavy boots.)

Dad: *Le voy a preguntar a la empleada si tienen tenis de los que quieres.*

(I'm going to ask the employee if they have the kind of sneakers you want).

The dad returned.

Dad: *Tienes razón, no tienen tenis blancos. Me dijo que fueramos a la tienda que está en el centro comercial a cinco minutos de aquí.*

(You're right, they don't have white sneakers. She told me to go to the store that's in the mall five minutes from here.)

Andrew: *Debemos ir ahí entonces.*

(We should go there then.)

Dad: *Si, vamos.*

(Yes, let's go.)

Andrew: *Espero que tengan un par. Si no – pues, no sé. No iré a la fiesta de Carla.*

(I hope they have a pair. If not, well, I don't know. I won't go to Carla's party.)

Dad: *No te preocupes, los vamos a encontrar. Ya verás.*

(Don't worry, we'll find them. You'll see.)

Scenario #3 - A Lost Jacket

Florence: *Permiso, señor, créo que olvidé mi chaqueta en la sala numbero dos. Es roja y la tela es de terciopelo. Es larga y tiene un collar dorado.*

(Excuse me, sir, I think I left my jacket in theater number two. It's red, and the cloth is velvet. It's long, and it has a golden collar.)

Security Guard: *Sí, se encontró una chaqueta parecida a su descripción y fue llevada al mostrador de ayuda. Estará ahí.*

(Yes, a jacket similar to your description was found and taken to the help desk. It'll be there.)

Florence: *¡Que bueno! ¡Muchísimas gracias.*
(That's great! Thank you tons.)

Security Guard: *Ni un problema, tenga buenos noches.*
(Not a problem, have a goodnight.)

3.3 Directions

Directions are essential for any excursion; one could be wandering the streets of Guadalajara in Mexico or looking for a clothing store through Brooklyn in New York City. Whatever the case may be, asking and giving directions is an important tool in any travel scenario. In past sections, we've taken a look at how to ask and answer questions, as well as take a look at example scenarios where the characters ask one another for directions. Inquiring about directions could be as simple as asking someone *¿dónde estoy?* (where am I?). In the following example scenarios, there will be many opportunities to sharpen the ability to ask and answer questions with ease.

Scenario #1 - Looking For Landmarks

Joel: *Hola señor, ¿me puede ayudar?*
(Hello sir, could you help me?)

Older Man: *Sí, ¿qué necesitas?*
(Yes, what do you need?)

Joel: *Estoy visitando Barcelona – solo soy un turista. Y estoy perdido tratando de llegar a Parc Guëll en tren. ¿Me podría ayudar, por favor?*
(I'm visiting Barcelona. I'm only a tourist, and I'm lost trying to reach Parc Guëll by train. Could you help me, please?

Older Man: *Sí, esta bien. Ahorita estamos en el barrio de Eixample. Caminarás por el Passeig de Gràcia y encontrarás la estación de Diagonal. Tomarás el metro yendo norte hacía Trinitat Nova. Te vas a vajar en la estación de Lesseps y caminarás por la Travessera de Dalt hasta llegar a la Carrer de*

Larrard. Continúa camindando norte y en cinco cuadras llegarás a Parc Güell.

(Yes, it's all good. Right now, we are in the Eixample neighborhood. You'll walk on the Passeig de Gràcia, and you'll find the Diagonal station. You'll take the metro going north toward Trinitat Nova. You'll get off at the Lesseps station, and you'll walk on the Travessera de Dalt until you reach Carrer de Larrard. Continue walking north, and in five blocks, you'll reach Parc Güell.)

Joel: *¡Muy amable! No le puedo agradecer suficiente. Entonces, ¿me vajaré en la estación de Lesseps?*

(You're so kind! I can't thank you enough. So, I'll get off at the Lesseps station?)

Older Man: *Sí, la Lesseps. También te puedes bajar el la estación de Vallcarca, pero tendras que caminar un poco más.*

(Yes, the Lesseps. You can also get off the Vallcarca station, but you will have to walk a little more.)

Joel: *Está bien. Voy a recordar todos los pasos.*
(Very well. I'll remember all the steps.)

Older Man: *Buena suerte. Nosotros decimos 'bona sort' en catalán.*
(Good luck. *We say 'bona sort' in Catalan.*)

Joel: *¿Cómo se diría 'muchas gracias' en catalán?*
(How would you say 'thank you so much' in Catalan?)

Older Man: *Decimos 'moltes gràcies.'*
(We say 'moltes gràcies.')

Joel: *¡Moltes gràcies! Adios, cuídese.*
(Moltes gràcies! Goodbye, take care.)

Older Man: *De res. ¡De nada!*
(De res. You're welcome!)

Scenario #2 - Looking For Parking

Sabrina: *Hey, ¡hola! Estoy buscando un aparcamiento que está en la escuina de la calle Libertad y la Guayaqui. ¿Sabes cómo llegar ahí de aquí?*

(Hey, hi! I'm looking for a parking lot that's in the corner of Libertad street and Guayaqui. Do you know how to get there from here?)

Pedestrian: *Sí, girá a la izquierda cuando llegues a la calle de Frugoni. Luego doblá a la derecha cuando mires la calle de Constituyente. Seguí manejando derecho y Constituyente se convertirá en la calle Canelones. Doblá a la izquierda cuando veas la calle Francisco Araúcho, despues haz una derecha en la avenida Rivera. Por último, doblás en la calle Pereira y rapidito vas a ver el aparcamiento.*

(Yes, make a left when you get to Frugoni street. Then turn right when you see Constituyente street. Keep driving straight, and Constituyente will become Canelos street. Make a left when you see Francisco Araúcho street, then make a right in Rivera avenue. Lastly, turn in Pereira street, and you'll quickly see the parking lot.)

Sabrina: *¡Suena bien! Muchas gracias, señor.*
(Sounds great! Thank you so much, sir.)

Pedestrian: *¡De nada!*
(You're welcome!)

Scenario #3 - Helping a Visitor

Stranger: *Permiso, ¿puedes hablar en español?*
(Pardon, can you speak Spanish?)

Dalia: *Sí, sí puedo. ¿Qué pasó?*
(Yes, yes I can. What's up?)

Stranger: *Estoy buscando el Empire State Building. ¿Cómo lo puedo encontrar?*

(I'm looking for the Empire State Building. How can I find it?)

Dalia: *Continúa caminando por la calle treinta y cuatro. Cuando llegues a la Quinta Avenida, vas a estar parada exactamente al lado del Empire State Building.*
(Continue walking on thirty-fourth street. When you get to Fifth Avenue, you'll be standing exactly next door to the Empire State Building.)

Stranger: *Muy bien, entonces ¿permanesco caminando en está calle?*
(Very good, so I just stay walking on this street?)

Dalia: *¡Sí! Si no te desviás de la calle treinta y cuatro, vas a llegar bien rápido.*
(Yes! If you don't deviate from thirty-fourth street, you'll get there very quickly.)

Stranger: *Está bien, ¡muchas gracias!*
(Okay, thank you very much!)

Dalia: *¡Si claro!*
(Yes, of course!)

3.4 Ordering Food & Drinks

Foods are another essential category in everyday living. Be it you're cooking at home or going out for a nice lunch, it's important to articulate all sorts of foods in all kinds of contexts. In this section, we'll continue building on the ability to express questions, answers, and commands in Spanish. The following example scenarios will feature new vocabulary words, as well as unseen nouns related to food, cooking, and drinks.

Scenario #1: - Making Breakfast

Matthew: *Buenos día, mi amor. Te estoy cocinando el desayuno.*
(Good morning, my love. I'm cooking your breakfast.)

Jennifer: *Qué lindo, y ¿qué cocinas?*
(That's sweet, and what are you cooking?)

Matthew: *Estoy haciendo pan tostado con aguacate, huevos estrellados con chilles verdes y cebollas, tocino de pavo al horno, una ensalada de frutas y café.*
(I'm making toasted bread with avocado, fried eggs with green peppers and onions, baked turkey bacon, a fruit salad, and coffee.)

Jennifer: *¡Suena delicióso! Y tú, ¿qué vas a beber con el desayuno?*
(Sounds delicious! And you, what will you drink with your breakfast?

Matthew: *Ya me hicé un batido de piña con banana. Lo hice con leche de almendra y le puse un poco de miel.*
(I already made a pineapple smoothie with banana. I made it with almond milk, and I put a little honey in it.)

Jennifer: *¡Sos todo un experto! ¿Necesitas ayuda para coninar algo?*
(You're such an expert! Do you need help cooking something?)

Matthew: *¿Le puédes echar sal y pimienta a tus huevos? No sabía si te gustarían con uno poco de sal o no.*
(Could you add salt and pepper to your eggs? I didn't know if you liked them with a little salt or not.)

Jennifer: *Yo lo hago. No te preocupes.*
(I'll do it. Don't worry.)

Matthew: *¡Gracias, Jen! Por sí quieres batido de frutas, yo te dejo en la licuadora.*
(Thank you, Jen. In case you want fruit smoothie, I'll leave you some in the blender.)

Jennifer: *Sí, yo quiero – se ve deliciosa. Gracias por todo, amor.*

(Yes, I want some — it looks delicious. Thank you for everything, love.)

Matthew: *¡De nada, bebé! Te quiero mucho.*
(You're welcome, babe! I love you.)

Jennifer: *Yo también.*
(Me too.)

Scenario #2 - Ordering Lunch

Waiter: *¿Ya están listos para pedir su comida?*
(Are you both ready to order your food?)

Ángel: *Sí, ya estamos listos. Yo quiero el pollo al horno, pero solo tráeme las pechugas. Tambien quiero la ensalada de zanahoria y brócoli. Y también quiero una orden de ensalada de papas.*
(Yes, we're ready. I want the baked chicken, but only bring me the breasts. I also want the carrot and broccoli salad. And I also want an order of potato salad.)

Waiter: *Muy bien, ¿y para usted, señor?*
(Very good, and for you, sir?)

Sebastían: *Solo quiero la sopa de vegetales con tofu hornado.*
(I only want the vegetable soup with baked tofu.)

Waiter: *Muy buena elección, señor. Entonces, para usted, el pollo hornado pero solo las pechugas, la ensalada de zanahoria y brócoli y la ensalada de papas. Y para usted, solamente la sopa de vegetales con el tofu hornado.*
(Very good choice, sir. So, for you, the baked chicken but only the chicken breasts, the carrot and broccoli salad, and the potato salad. And for you, only the vegetable soup with baked tofu.)

Ángel: *Perfecto. También quiero una copa de vino blanco.*
(Perfect. I also want a glass of white wine.)

Sebastían: *Y yo quiero una taza de jugo de granada y naranja.*
(And I want a glass of pomegranate and orange juice.)

Waiter: *Muy bien, ahorita pondré sus ordenes y traeré las bebidas. ¿Les gustaría pan para la mesa?*
(Very good, I'll place your orders, and bring the drinks right away. Would you like some bread for the table?)

Ángel: *Muchas gracias, y sí, por favor.*
(Thank you very much, and yes, please.)

Sebastían: *Sí, y mantequilla, por favor.*
(Yes, and some butter, please.)

Waiter: *Excelente, ya regreso.*
(Excellent, I'll be right back.)

Ángel: *Muchas gracias.*
(Thank you very much.)

Sebastían: *Sí, gracias.*
(Yes, thank you.)

Scenario #3 - Going to a Fast Food Place

Luke: *Hola, ¿puedo tener el número cuatro, pero sin tocino? También quiero unas papas fritas y una soda mediana.*
(Hi, can I have a number four, but without bacon? Y also want some french fries and a medium soda.)

Cashier: *Lastimosamente, la máquina de refrescos no está funcionando. Solo tenemos limonada y agua.*
(Unfortunately, the soda machine isn't working. We only have lemonade and water.)

Luke: *Bueno, en vez de la soda, quiero una limonada mediana.*
(Okay, instead of the soda, I want a medium lemonade.)

Cashier: *Muy bien, ¿eso será toda su orden?*
(Very good, will that be your whole order?)

Luke: *Sí, eso es todo.*
    (Yes, that's all.)

Cashier: *Su total es de $6.25. ¿Pagará con tarjeta o efectivo?*
    (Your total is $6.25. Will you pay with card or cash?)

Luke: *Con efectivo. Aquí está.*
    (With cash. Here you go.)

Cashier: *¡Gracias!*
    (Thank you!)

3.5 Work & Studies

Work and schoolwork are a daily reality for most. From office work and chemistry presentations to accounting reports and English essays, work is a key part of the day. Millions of people do not only work or study in their hometowns and cities; they also venture out across the world and work internationally. So many people migrate to places like Madrid, Spain and Mexico City to find work and invent a new life in Ibero-America. In this section, we'll focus on work-related and school-related terms and conversations. Similar to previous sections, new vocabulary will be introduced, and it's important to pay close attention to it.

Scenario #1 - The Work Meeting

Emma: *Buenos días a todos. Cómo ya sabemos, hoy hablaremos sobre el evento especial que tendremos la otra semana. Me gustaría saber cómo le va a todo el mundo, y sí alguien necesita ayuda, por favor, hágamelo saber. Daniel, ¿cómo te va con los refrescos y las bebidas?*
    (Good morning, everyone. As you all know, today we'll talk about the special event we're having next week. I would like to know how everyone is doing, and if somebody needs help, please, let me know. Daniel, how are you doing with the refreshments and drinks?)

Daniel: *Muy bien, toda la comida ya está lista y pagada.*
    (Very well, all the food is ready and paid for.)

Ian: *El lugar del evento también ya está reservado. Tenemos todas las mesas y asientos listos para la otra semana.*
(The event venue is also reserved. We have all the tables and seats ready for next week.)

Zoe: *Ya contacté las oficinas de Houston y Dallas, y ambas me dejaron saber que la mayoría de los empleados llegarán.*
(I already contacted the Houston and Dallas offices, and they both told me that most of the employees would come.)

Amy: *Envié el informe de costos al departamento de contabilidad. Les hice saber que no excidimos nuestro presupuesto.*
(I sent the costs report to the accounting department. I let them know that we didn't exceed our budget.)

Emma: *¡Qué trabajo tan excelente! Entonces ya estamos listos para nuestro evento.*
(What an excellent job! Then we are ready for our event.)

Ian: *Sí, la planificación fue impecable.*
(Yes, the planning went impeccably.)

Zoe: *Espero qué todo salga de acierdo al plan.*
(I hope everything goes according to plan.)

Daniel: *Todo irá bien, ya veremos.*
(Everything will go well; we'll see.)

Emma: *Buen trabajo para todos. Ya podemos terminar la reunión.*
(Good job, everyone. We can finish the meeting.)

Scenario #2 - A Busy College Week

Mario: *Bianca, ¿comenzastes el ensayo de inglés?*
(Bianca, did you start the English essay?)

Bianca: *No, aún no. ¿Cuándo es el plazo para del ensayo?*

(No, not yet. When is the deadline for the essay?)

Mario: *El dieciocho de febrero a la medianoche.*
(February 18th at midnight.)

Bianca: *Gracias por recordarme. He estado bien ocupada terminando mi taréa de matemática y de química. Y todavía tengo que terminar mi solicitud para estudiar en el extranjero.*
(Thanks for reminding me. I've been very busy finishing my math and chemistry homework. And I still have to finish my application to study abroad.)

Mario: *Sí, terminando tanto trabajo requiere bastante tiempo. ¡Y qué bien! ¿Dónde quieres estudiar?*
(Yes, finishing so much work requires a lot of time. And that's great! Where do you want to study?)

Bianca: *El programa es en Grecia y dura tre meses. ¡Estoy bien emocionada!*
(The program is in Greece and lasts three months. I'm very excited!)

Mario: *¿Cómo terminarás toda tu tarea, el ensayo de inglés y también la solicitud para el programa en Grecia?*
(How will you finish all your homework, the English essay, and also the application for the program in Greece?)

Bianca: *Con paciencia y determinación. Mi consejera academica me está ayudando con el proceso de la solicitud.*
(With patience and determination. My academic counselor is helping me with the application process.)

Mario: *Qué bien. Si necesitas ayuda con el ensayo, yo te puedo ayudar.*
(That's great. If you need help with the essay, I can help you.)

Bianca: *¡Muchas gracias, Mario! Me tengo que ir a mi clase de historia. Te miró en la noche con Noa para estudiar para el examen de biología.*

(Thank you so much, Mario! I have to go to my history class. I'll see you tonight with Noa to study for our biology exam.)

Mario: *¡Suena bien! Te miro en la noche.*
(Sounds good! I'll see you tonight.)

Bianca: *¡Cuídate! Adios.*
(Take care! Bye.)

Mario: *Adios, Bianca.*
(Bye, Bianca.)

Scenario #3 - Assigning a Test

Pablo: *¡Clase! No se les olvide que para mañana tienen que terminar le lectura de esta semana.*
(Class! Don't forget that for tomorrow you must finish the reading.)

Felipe: *Profesor, ¿tendremos un examen hacerca de los capítulos de la semana?*
(Professor, will we have a test based on the chapters of this week?)

Pablo: *Sí, Felipe. Tendremos un examen. Resumen sus notas, por favor.*
(Yes, Felipe. We will have a test. Review your notes, please.)

Felipe: *Bueno, gracias profesor.*
(Okay, thank you, professor.)

Pablo: *Claro.*
(Of course.)

3.6 Celebrations, Going Out, & Partying

Going out on a Friday night with friends is an exceptional experience. Everyone wishes to wind down with loved ones, friends, and co-workers after a hard week of labor. Celebrations can rejuvenate the spirit and re-energize the body, be it a weekend outing, a holiday party, or a simple get-together. Partying is huge among Spaniards and Latin Americans; in Spanish culture, there is no greater joy than spending quality time partying with friends until 6 AM, enjoying some great music and wonderful company. In this section, we'll explore some example scenarios that detail the celebrations of a variety of figures and how they plan together to make it all happen. Pay close attention to new vocabulary words, as there will be a few.

Scenario #1 - The Preparation

Isabel: *Valerie, ¿vas a ir a la fiesta de Rodrigo?*
    (Valerie, are you going to Rodrigo's party?)

Valerie: *Sí, tengo planes de ir. ¿Y tú vas también?*
    (Yes, I have plans to go. Are you also going?)

Isabel: *Aún no lo sé todavía. Ni sé qué me pondría para el evento.*
    (I don't know yet. I don't even know what I would wear to the event.)

Valerie: *Ponte un vestido negro simple y ya. ¡Ven! Estará bien divertido. Todo el mundo en la oficina va ir.*
    (Just put on a simple black dress and there. Come! It'll be really fun. Everyone in the office is coming.)

Isabel: *Tienes razón, no me quiero perder la noche. ¿Cómo te vestirás para la fiesta?*
    (You're right; I don't want to miss the night. How will you dress for the party?)

Valerie: *¡Eso es lo que me gusta escuchar! Me pondré un vestido rojo y unos tacones negros. Me veré simple y elegante.*
    (That's what I like to hear! I'll wear a red dress and some black heels. I'll look simple and elegant.)

Isabel: *¡Me encanta! La noche será fenomenal. Le haré saber a Rodrigo que sí iré a su fiesta.*

(I love it! The night will be phenomenal. I'll let Rodrigo know that I will go to his party.)

Valerie: *¡Fabuloso! Te veré más tarde, entonces.*
(Fabulous! I'll see you later, then.)

Isabel: *¡Ciao, amiga!*
(Bye, friend!)

Valerie: *Ciao, Isabel. ¡Besitos!*
(Bye, Isabel. Kisses!)

Scenario #2 - An Ask for Help

Alexander: *¿Aló? ¿Bruno?*
(Hello? Bruno?)

Bruno: *Hola, Alex. ¿Qué tal?*
(Hey, Alex. What's up?)

Alexander: *Hola chico. Te llamo porque le voy hacer una fiesta de sorpresa a Lea y necesito tú ayuda.*
(Hey, dude. I'm calling you because I'm making a surprise party for Lea, and I need your help.)

Bruno: *Sí, está bien. ¿Cómo puedo ayudarte?*
(Yes, that's fine. How can I help you?)

Alexander: *Necesito que compres la cervezas y pizzas para comer. Yo conseguiré los globos, los invitados y la música.*
(I need you to get the beers and pizza to eat. I'll get the balloons, the guests, and the music.)

Bruno: *¡Suena genial! ¿A qué hora comenzará la fiesta?*
(Sounds great! At what time will the party begin?)

Alexander: *Comenzará a las nueve y mieda de la noche.*
(It'll start at 9:30 PM.)

Bruno: *¡Okay! Llegaré con unas bebidas y la comida.*

(Okay! I'll arrive with some drinks and food.)

Alexander: *Genial, te veo en un ratito.*
(Great, see you in a little bit.)

Bruno: *Bueno, ¡adios chico!*
(Great, bye dude.)

Scenario #3 - Ordering At the Bar

Julia: *Hola, barman, ¿puedo tener una margarita de fresa con sal en el borde del vaso, por favor?*
(Hey, bartender, could I have a strawberry margarita with salt on the glass' rim, please?

Hernán: *Yo quiero un chupito de vodka y una rodaja de limón. Gracias.*
(I want a shot of vodka and and slice of lemon. Thank you.)

Bartender: *¿Eso será todo?*
(Will that be all?)

Julia: *También queremos una orden de los nachos con pollo. Otra amiga va a llegar en unos minutos, así que volveremos a pedir más comida y otras bebidas.*
(We also want an order of nachos with chicken. Another friend will arrive here in a few minutes, so we're going to order additonal food and drinks.)

Bartender: *Muy bien, ahorita les hago las bebidas. También les pediré la orden de los nachos.*
(Very good, I'll make you the drinks right away. I'll also put in the order for nachos.)

Hernán: *Muchas gracias.*
(Thank you so much.)

Julia: *¡Sí, gracias!*
(Yes, thank you!)

Chapter 4 - Spanish Phrases III: Important Terms

4.1 Shopping

Shopping may be one of the most popular leisure activities in the world. Everyone loves to go to the mall or an outlet and hunt for deals. The best offers are always around the corner. In the United States, purchasing goods is a foundation of the economy; with shopping extravaganzas such as Black Friday, Labor Day, and, in some cases, Christmas in July, everyone always has the opportunity to buy a new dryer or snatch a new technological device. In this section, we will explore and understand important terms and phrases to memorize when it comes to shopping. The table below will highlight important vocabulary words to know. Following the table, example scenarios will place the phrases and terms into context.

Shopping: What to Know

The table below features some necessary terms and phrases to understand when doing shopping-related activities. Many vocabulary words may have appeared in previous sections, but it's still necessary to emphasize their importance:

Shopping Terms
horarió de operación   (business hours)
la tienda   (the store)
el supermercado   (the supermarket)

el centro comercial
(the mall)
una oferta
(an offer/a sale)
¿cuánto cuesta?
(how much is it?)
¿puedo probarmeló/probarmelá?
(can I try it on?/can I try it on? (feminine))
la talla
(the size)
está abierto
(it's open)
está cerrado
(it's close)
la entrada
(the entrance)
la salida
(the exit)

Scenario #1 - Finding a Clothing Store

Daniela: *¿Sabes dónde podemos encontrar pantalones baratos?*
(Do you know where we can find cheap pants?)

Isaac: *Podríamos ir a la tienda de ropa que está al lado de los lugares para comer.*
(We could go to the clothing store that's next to the food places.)

Sara: *¡Mami! ¡Papi! Yo quieró un vestido, no unos pantalones.*
(Mommy! Daddy! I want a dress, not a pair of pants.)

Daniela: *Mi amor, sí encontramos pantalones en oferta, también te podríamos comprar un vestido bien bonito. ¿Cómo te suena eso?*
(My love, if we find discounted pants, we could also buy a very nice dress. How does that sound to you?)

Sara: *¡Suena muy bien! Quieró un vestido con rosas pequeñas.*
(It sounds great! I want a dress with small roses.)

Isaac: *Está bien, hijita. Daniela, mira, esa tienda dice 'cincuenta por ciento de descuento en todo.'*
(Okay, baby daughter. Daniela, look, that store says 'fifty percent off everything.')

Daniela: *Entremos ahí — yo sé que encontraremos algo muy bonito para Sara.*
(Let's go in there — I know we'll find something very nice for Sara.)

After searching through the store.

Isaac: *Mira este par de pantalones de jean. ¿Crees qué le quepan a Sara?*
(Look at this pair of jean pants. Do you think they'll fit Sara?)

Daniela: *Sí, sí le van a quedar. ¿Cuanto cuestan?*
(Yes, yes they'll fit her. How much are they?)

Isaac: *Tienen un descuento de ciencuenta por ciento. Entonces, van a constar...$12.*
(They have a 50% off discount. So, they'll cost...$12.)

Daniela: *¡Estan baratísimos! Mi amor, te compraremos el vestido.*
(They're so cheap! My love, we'll buy you the dress.)

Sara: *¡Estoy feliz! ¡Gracias, mami! ¡Gracias, papi!*
(I'm happy! Thank you, mommy! Thank you, daddy!)

Isaac: *De nada, mi amor. Vamos a buscarte el vestido bonito.*
(You're welcome, my love. Let's go find you a pretty dress.)

Sara: *¡Que bien!*
(So cool!)

Scenario #2: A Search at the Supermarket

Samantha: *Con permiso, señorita, ando buscando cerezas y ceral para niños. ¿Dónde los puedo encontrar?*
(Pardon, miss, I'm looking for cherries and kid cereals. Where can I find them?)

Employee: *Las cerezas están en el pasillo número uno. Los cereales estarán en el pasillo número cinco, al lado de las comidas secas. Si necesita ayuda adicional, solo avísele a un empleado.*
(The cherries are in aisle number one. The cereals will be in aisle number five, next to the dry foods. If you need additional help, just let an employee know.)

Samantha: *Muchas gracias. Perdon, ¿y dónde puedo encontrar las manzanas verdes?)*
(Thank you very much. Sorry, where can I find green apples?)

Employee: *También estan en el pasillo número uno, cerca de la entrada del supermercado.*
(They're also in aisle number one, near the supermarket entrance.)

Samantha: *¡Muchísimas, gracias!*
(Thank you very much!)

Employee: *De nada, señora.*
(You're welcome, ma'am.)

Scenario #3 - The Wrong Size

Camilo: *Disculpa, chico. Esta camiseta no me queda bien. ¿Me podrías traer una talla más grande?*
Sorry, young man. This shirt doesn't fit me well. Could you bring me a bigger size?)

Employee: *Sí, claro. ¿Qué talla es esta?*
(Yes, of course. What size is this?)

Camilo: *Es una pequeña. Tráeme una mediana — no, ¿sabes qué? Tráeme una grande también, por cualquier cosa.*
(It's small. Bring me a medium — no, you know what? Bring me a large, just in case.)

Employee: *Una mediana y una grande — ya vuelvo.*
A medium and a large —I'll be right back.

Camilo: *Gracias.*
(Thank you.)

4.2 Travel, Tourism, & Transportation

Travel is universal. Everyone experiences journeys, be it a morning commute to work or an international excursion to another continent. When traveling abroad, there's a fresh novelty to every place you visit. As a tourist, you have the ability to surround yourself in a new culture and learn new perspectives; the premise of a tourist is not only to relax but also to reimagine themselves and the world around them. Whether you're traveling by train, boat, car, or plane, something new will await you on the other side. For example, when traveling to South America, anybody will feel welcomed and cared for by kind, open-hearted people. In this section, we will explore and understand important terms and phrases to memorize when it comes to traveling and transportation. The table below will highlight important vocabulary words to know. Following the graphic, example scenarios will place the phrases and terms into context.

Travel 101: Tourism and Navigation

The table below features some necessary terms and phrases to understand when traveling both within and outside the country. Many vocab words may have appeared in previous sections, but it's still necessary to emphasize their importance:

Traveling Terms
un avión   (a plane)
un pasajero/una pasajera   (a passenger/a passenger (feminine))
Un vuelo   (a flight)
el airopuerto   (the airport)
el equipaje   (the luggage)
una escala   (a layover)

un boleto
(a ticket)
un turista
(a tourist)
el tren
(the train)
una estación
(a station)
un taxi
(a taxi)
un autobus
(a bus)
un barco
(a boat)
la destinación
(the destination)
¿a qué hora sale/llega el ____?)
(at what time does ____ leave/arrive?)
¿dónde está ____?
(where is ____?)

Scenario #1 - A Parisian Flight

Ben: *¿A qué hora sale tu vuelo a París?*
(At what time does your flight to Paris leave?)

Sandra: *A las seis y media de la noche. El vuelo durará ocho horas, pero aún asi, tengo una escala en Ginebra, Suiza.*
(At 6:30 PM. The flight will last eight hours, but still, I have a layover in Geneva, Switzerland.)

Ben: *¿Cuanto tiempo se tardará la escala en Ginebra?*
(How long will the layover in Geneva take?)

Sandra: *Dos horas. De ahí, mi vuelo hacia París partirá a las nueve y cuarto de la mañana, tiempo local.*
(Two hours. From there, my flight to Paris will depart at 9:15 AM, local time.)

Ben: *Muy bien. ¿Tienes todo listo: tu pasaporte, tus medicamentos, tu boleto — todo?*
(Very good. Do you have everything prepared: your passport, your medication, your ticket — everything?)

Sandra: *Sí, lo tengo todo en mi equipaje de mano. Estoy lista.*
(Yes, I have everything in my carry-on luggage)

Ben: *Brillante. Llámame cuando vayas en el taxi del aeropuerto Charles De Gaulle al hotel. Esperaré tu llamada.*
(Brilliant. Call me when you're on the taxi from the Charles De Gaulle airport to the hotel. I'll wait for your call.)

Sandra: *Está bien, Ben, yo te llamaré. Y también te compraré unos chocolates suizos por mientras espero mi vuelo a Francia.*
(Okay, Ben, I'll call you. And I'll also buy you some Swiss chocolates while I wait for my flight to France.)

Ben: *Qué linda, muchas gracias.*
(So sweet, thank you.)

Sandra: *Bueno, llegué a mi terminal. Te voy a dejar, ¿okay? Te llamo cuando pase por el TSA.*
(Alright, I arrived at my terminal. I'm going to hang up, okay? I'll call you after I pass the TSA.)

Ben: *Te quiero mucho, Sandra. Cuídate.*
(I love you, Sandra. Take care.)

Sandra: *Tú tambien. ¡Te quiero mucho, ciao!*
(You too. I love you. Bye!)

Scenario #2 - Tourists in Buenos Aires

Emmanuel: *Para llegar a la Plaza del Congreso, ¿qué crees qué seria mejor: irnos caminando o por taxi?*
(To get to the Congreso Plaza, what do you think would be better: going on foot or by taxi?)

Rafaela: *Siento que caminando nos tardariamos demasiado. Se ve lejos.*
(I feel like walking would take us too long. It looks far.)

Emmanuel: *Sí, tienes razón. También podriamos tomar el tren hacia el centro de la ciudad.*
(Yeah, you're right. We could also take the train toward the city center.)

Rafaela: *Prefiero el taxi. Más rápido y más seguro. ¿Tienes efectivo para evitar pagar con la tarjeta de crédito?*
(I prefer a taxi. It's faster and safer. Do you have some cash to avoid paying with the credit card?)

Emmanuel: *Sí, tengo suficiente efectivo para hoy.*
(Yeah, I have enough cash for today?)

Rafaela: *Me encanta. ¿Tienes la botella de agua contigo?*
(I love it. Do you the water bottle with you?)

Emmanuel: *¡Sí! Estamos listos.*
(Yes! We're ready.)

Rafaela: *¡Vámonos!*
(Let's go!)

Scenario #3: Staten Island Ride

Amanda: *Señor, disculpe. ¿Aquí se agarra el barco a Staten Island?*
(Sir, excuse me. Is this where I catch the boat to Staten Island?

Stranger: *¡Sí! Sale en diez minutos — llegaste a tiempo.*
(Yeah! It leaves in ten minutes — you arrived on time.)

Amanda: *¡Estupendo! ¡Muchas gracias!*
(Great! Thank you so much!)

4.3 Money & Economy

Money permeates all aspects of society. Not only does currency allow us to trade, it allows us to establish a home, a career, and to gain comfort. Credit cards, savings accounts, and loans — money opens the door to a myriad of financial operations. Buying a small coffee every day is as impactful as trading bonds in the stock market; capital grows and declines but is ever-changing in the modern world. That is the only certainty of money: it never stops moving. Having money to withdraw to purchase groceries or travel to Brazil gives any of us financial ability to live secure lives. In this section, we will explore and understand important terms and phrases to memorize when it comes to finances and the economy. The table below will highlight important vocabulary words to know. Following this are example scenarios that will place the phrases and terms into context.

Money & Finances: Money Talks — in Spanish

The table below features some necessary terms and phrases to know when dealing with or speaking about financial and economic circumstances and topics.

Financial and Economic Terms:
interés
(interest)
una acción
(a share/a stock)
bolsa de comercio
(stock market)
crédito
(credit)
un préstamo
(a loan)
cuenta de ahorros
(savings account)
cuenta de cheques
(checkings account)
valor
(value)
balance
(balance)
un banco
(a bank)

billetes   (banknotes)
cambio de divisas   (currency exchange)
una cuota   (an installment)
la economía   (the economy)
salario   (wage)
aumentar   (increase)
disminuir   (decrease)
transacción de valores   (transaction of values)

Scenario #1: Opening a Checkings Account

Bank Teller: *Hola, bienvenida al banco. ¿Cómo la pudemos ayudar?*

(Hello, welcome to the bank. How can we help you?)

Valentina: *Hola, buenos días. Me acabo de mudar a Madrid y me gustaría abrir una cuenta de cheques. Tengo todos los documentos necesarios para el trámite.*

(Hi, good morning. I just moved to Madrid, and I would like to open a checking account. I have all the necessary documents for the process.)

Bank Teller: *Muy bien, esto solo se tomará unos minutos. Necesito su pasaporte, su tarjeta de identificación, comprobante de residencia en España y un mínimo de ciento cincuenta euros.*

(Alright, this will only take a few minutes. I need your passport, your identification card, proof of residence in Spain, and a minimum of €150.)

Valentina: *Sí, por supuesto. Aquí estan todos los documentos — también tengo un cheque de docientos euros.*

(Yes, of course. Here are all the documents — I also have a check for €200.)

Bank Teller: *Muy bien, solo deme unos minutos y le abriré la cuenta con el banco.*

(Very well, just give me a few minutes, and I'll open your account with the bank.)

Valentina: *Muchas gracias.*

(Thank you so much.)

Bank Teller: *Claro. ¿Está interesada en abrir una cuenta de ahorros también?*

(Of course. Are you interested in opening a savings account also?)

Valentina: *No, gracias. Solo la de cheques por hoy.*

(No, thank you. Only the one for checkings for today.)

Bank Teller: *Muy bien. Ya regreso, le traeré su nueva tarjeta de débito.*
(Very good. I'll be right back; I'll bring you your new debit card.)

Valentina: *Sí, tome su tiempo.*
(Yes, take your time.)

Bank Teller: *Aquí esta su nueva tarjeta y un paquete con toda la información de su nueva cuenta. ¡Bienvenida a la familia del banco!*
(Here is your new card and a packet with all your new account information. Welcome to the bank's family!)

Valentina: *Muchísimas gracias. ¡Qué tenga un bien día!*
(Thank you a lot. Hope you have a nice day!)

Bank Teller: *¡Gracias, igualmente!...Puedo aydar a la próxima visita.*
(Thanks, you as well!...I can help the next guest.)

Scenario #2 - On the Economy

Vanessa: *¿Has visto las noticias sobre el crecimiento de trabajos del país?*
(Have you seen the news about the job increase in the country?)

Nelson: *No, en realidad no le he prestado atención. ¿Cuáles son las novedades?*
(No, I really haven't paid attention to it. What is the news?)

Vanessa: *La tasa de desempleo es de tres punto cinco por ciento.*
(The unemployment rate is at 3.5%)

Nelson: *Wow, ¿alguna vez ha sido tan baja?*

(Wow, has it ever been that low?)

Vanessa: *No, por eso es tan emocionante. La economía está muy bien —es saludable.*
(No, that's why it's so exciting. The economy is doing very well —it's healthy.)

Nelson: *Esperemos que siga así.*
(Let's hope it'll stay that way.)

Vanessa: *Sí, esperemos que sí.*
(Yeah, let's hope so.)

Scenario #3 - Diversifying Finances

Julian: *Quiero diversificar mi cartera financiera.*
(I want to diversify my financial portfolio.)

Charles: *Deberías de comprar más acciones preferidas. Tienen más valor que acciones comunes.*
(You should buy more preferred stocks. They have more value than common stocks.)

Julian: *Suenan interesantes, las examinaré más a fondo.*
(They sound interesting; I'll look further into them.)

4.4 Communication, Media, & the Internet

Telecommunications have changed the world around us. It's now possible to live in Oregon and have friends who reside in Cairo, Egypt, or who work in Auckland, New Zealand. In the last decade, applications, websites, and social media platforms revolutionized how human beings communicate and interact with one another; the world is now just a few taps away. The Internet itself has democratized information and transformed old industries while introducing new forms of labor, such as digital design and IT professions. Of course, the smartphone, the post child of the Internet era, has been described as a magical device that connected humanity to itself. In this section, we will explore important terms and phrases that deal with the communication landscape, including apps, online platforms, and the Internet. The table below will highlight important vocabulary words to know. Following the table, example scenarios will place the phrases and terms into context.

Communication Galore

The table below features some necessary terms and phrases to know when discussing communication-related topics, both in real life and online.

Communication-Based Terms
una aplicación/un app
(an application/an app)
redes sociales
(social media)
un teléfono inteligente
(a smartphone)
una computadora
(a computer)
una página web
(a website)
el navegador
(the browser)
el correo electrónico
(email)
la contraseña
(the password)

googlear (to Google)	
descargar (download)	
la portada (the homepage)	
el internet (the Internet)	
el wifi (Wi-Fi)	
un video (a video)	
una foto (a photo)	
streaming, i.e. streaming música, videos (streaming/streaming music/streaming videos)	
una conversación (a conversation)	
mensajes privados (private messages)	
Instagram, Facebook, Twitter, WhatsApp (Instagram, Facebook, Twitter, WhatsApp)	

Scenario #1 - Social Media Acquaintances

Stephanie: *Kathy, ¿seguís a Ryan Harper en Instagram?*
(Kathy, do you follow Ryan Harper on Instagram?)

Kathy: *Creó qué no. ¿Quién es Ryan Harper?*
(I don't think so. Who's Ryan Harper?)

Stephanie: *Èl estuvo en nuestra clase de sociología urbana. Pero en fin, los dos nos seguimos en Instagram y hace dos días me mandó un mensaje privado.*
(He was in our urban sociology class. But anyway, we both follow each other on Instagram, and two days ago, he sent me a private message.)

Kathy: *¿Qué te dijo?*
(What did he say to you?)

Stephanie: *Qué cuando él regrese del Reinó Unido, deberíamos de conseguir un café juntos.*
(That when he returns from the United Kingdom, we should get a cup of coffee together.)

Kathy: *¿Ustedes eran amigos? Ósea, ¿sé hablaban en la clase?*
(Were you guys friends? Like, did you talk to one another in class?)

Stephanie: *Sí, hablábamos de vez en cuando. Pero no era una amistad de verdad. Sólo nos seguimos en nuestras redes sociales.*
(Yeah, we spoke every once in a while. But it wasn't a true friendship. We just follow each other on our social media.)

Kathy: *Salí con él — ¿quién sabe? Tal vez se gustan o se convierten amigos. Contéstale el mensaje.*
(Go out with him — who knows? You might like each other or become friends. Respond to his message.)

Stephanie: *Tienes razón. Le mandaré un mensaje.*
(You're right. I'll send him a message.)

Kathy: *¡Buena suerte!*
(Good luck!)

Scenario #2: Upgrading Software

Elizabeth: *Hijo, ¿me puedes hacer un favor?*
(Son, can you do me a favor?)

Julián: *Sí, mamá, ¿cómo te ayudo?*
(Yeah, mom, how can I help you?)

Elizabeth: *Mi computadora recibió una notificación diciendo que tengo que actualizar el sistema operativo.*
(My computer received a notification saying that I have to upgrade the operating system.)

Julián: *Mi laptop recibió una notificación similar. ¿Necesitas ayuda actualizando tu computadora?*
(My laptop received a similar notification. Do you need help updating your computer?)

Elizabeth: *Sí, por favor, hijo. Gracias por ayudarme.*
(Yes, please, son. Thank you for helping me.)

Julián: *Está bien, mamá. Yo te aviso cuando tu computadora termine de descargar la actualización de seguridad.*
(It's okay, mom. I'll let you know when your computer is done downloading the security update.)

Elizabeth: *¡Gracias!*
(Thank you!)

Scenario #3 - Finding Wi-Fi

Martin: *Perdon, joven, ¿cuál es la contraseña para el wifi?*
(Pardon, young man, what's the password for the Wi-Fi?)

Barista: *La contraseña es "cielo987". "Cielo" escrito con una "c".*
(The password is "cielo987." "Cielo" spelled with a "c."

Martin: *Muchas gracias. ¿Por cuánto tiempo puedo usar el servicio de wifi?*

    (Thank you so much. For how long can I use the Wi-Fi service?)

Barista: *Por el tiempo que quiera. No hay limite.*

    (For how long you want. There's no limit.)

Martin: *¡Excelente! Muy amables. Voy a poder terminar todo mi trabajo.*

    (Excellent! Very kind. I'll be able to finish all my work.)

Barista: *¡Que lo disfrute!*

    (Enjoy it!)

4.5 Music

Music, many people say, is the language of the soul. Across the globe, there is an infinite spectrum of music that includes bands and orchestras, folk singers and pop stars, guitar players, and heavy metal artists. Instruments themselves are fixtures in the arts and a common staple in many societies; from oriental to western cultures, music sparkles with the uniqueness of the people. Music entails many things: genres, styles, compositions, theories, singers, and much more. In this section, we will explore important terms and phrases that deal with the musical landscape. The table below will highlight important vocabulary words to know. After this, the example scenarios will place the phrases and terms into context.

Music & It's Many Forms

The table below features some necessary terms and phrases to know when discussing music-related topics.

Musical Terms
la música (music)
una banda (a band)
el coro (the chorus)
un cantante (a singer)
la voz (the voice)
una canción (a song)
cantar (sing)
un concierto (a concert)
género musical

(musical genre)
la simfonía   (the symphony)
alternativa, blues, clásica, country, hip-hop   (alternative, blues, classical, country, hip-hop)
jazz, metal, el rap, rock, pop   (jazz, heavy metal, rap, rock, pop)
un instrumento   (an instrument)
el teclado   (the keyboard)
los tambores   (the drums)
la trompeta   (the trumpet)
el violín   (the violin)
el bajo   (the base)

Scenario #1 - Everyone Has a Favorite

Sam: *¿Cuál es tu género musical favorito?*
(What's your favorite musical genre?)

George: *No tengo solo uno, me gustan varios géneros musicales.*
(I don't have just one; I like multiple musical genres.)

Sam: *¿Cómo cuales?*
(Like which ones?)

George: *Me gusta la música rock, el alternativo, el jazz, el pop y la música clásica. Me encanta la variedad musical.*
(I like rock music, alternative, jazz, pop, and clasical music. I love musical variety.)

Sam: *Eso es interesante. Me gusta la musica alternativa también – es mi favorita.*
(That's interesting. I like alternative music too – it's my favorite.)

George: *¿Cuál es tu banda alternativa favorita?*
(What's your favorite alternative band?)

Sam: *Se llaman 'Sombras de Playa'. ¿Y la tuya?*
(They're called 'Beach Shadows.' And yours?)

George: *Mi banda favorita se llama 'Foster'. Son de Inglaterra.*
(My favorite band is called 'Foster.' They're from England.)

Sam: *¡A mi también me gustan Foster!*
(I like Foster too!)

George: *¿De verdad? Qué casualidad — soy un gran fan de Foster.*
(Really? What a coincidence — I'm a huge fan of Foster.)

Sam: *¡Sí! ¡Esto es genial! Amo todas sus canciones.*

(Yeah! This is great! I love all their songs.)

George: *¡Esto es asombroso! Me alegra que hayamos hablado de música.*
(This is awesome! I'm glad we talked about music.)

Sam: *Definitivamente.*
(Definitely.)

Scenario #2: Tonight's Concert

Celia: *Armond, ¿Vas a hacer algo en la noche?*
(Armond, are you doing something tonight?)

Armond: *No, en realidad qué no. ¿Por qué?*
(No, not really. Why?)

Celia: *Voy a ir a un concierto de rock con Taylor. ¿Quiéres ir con nosotras?*
(I'm going to a rock concert with Taylor. Do you want to come with us?)

Armond: *¿Dónde será el concierto?*
(Where will the concert be?)

Celia: *En la Fábrica de Rock. Ali iba ir con nosotras pero ya no puede, así que nos dio su boleto.*
(In Rock Factory. Ali was going to go with us, but he can't anymore, so he gave us his ticket.)

Armond: *¿Tengo que pagar por el boleto?*
(Do I have to pay for the ticket?)

Celia: *No, te lo damos porque sabemos que te encantan los conciertos de rock.*
(No, we're giving it to you because we know you love rock concerts.)

Armond: *¡Suena increíble! Por supuesto que iré. ¡Muchas gracias!*

(Sounds incredible! Of course, I'll go. Thank you so much!)

Celia: *¡Qué bien! El concierto comienza a las ocho y media de la noche, así que prepárate porque te recogeremos a las ocho en punto.*
(That's awesome! The concert starts at 8:30 PM, so be ready because we'll pick you up at eight on the dot.)

Armond: *¡Estaré listo!*
(I'll be ready!)

Scenario #3 - Instrument Lessons

Connie: *Mamá, para Navidad, me gustaría recibir un piano y un tutor para aprender a tocarlo.*
(Mom, for Christmas, I would like to receive a piano and a tutor to learn how to play it.)

Mom: *¿Y por qué el piano? ¿Por qué no la guitarra? ¿O la flauta?*
(And why the piano? Why not the guitar? Or the flute?)

Connie: *El piano es hermoso y quiero aprender a tocar música clásica.*
(The piano is beautiful, and I want to learn to play classical music.)

Mom: *Lo pensaré, pero no te haré ninguna promesa.*
(I'll think about it, but I won't make you any promises.)

Connie: *¡Gracias, mami!*
(Thank you, mommy!)

4.6 Sports

Sports may be the world's favorite pastime. The passion for both competition and sportsmanship is one carries pride and celebration across the globe. Every nation, every culture, and every community cherishes a sport, be it basketball or football.

Thousands gather in stadiums to watch a friendly match between old rivals; millions watch from their living rooms and bedrooms to experience the triumph or bitterness of their own favorite teams. In Spanish culture, football, what Americans know as soccer, is an incredibly beloved sport by both Spaniards and Latin Americans. Football runs deep in the blood of its many fans, and because of this, sports are a vital foundation in Ibero-America. In this section, we will explore the important terms and phrases that relate to the field of sports. The table below will highlight important vocabulary words to know. Following this, example scenarios will place the phrases and terms into context.

Sports for the Win

The table below features some necessary terms and phrases to know when discussing sports-related topics.

Sports Terms
los deportes (sports)
jugar (to play)
correr (to run)
nadar (to swim)
la cancha (the field/the court)
la piscina (the pool)

el estadio
(the stadium)
el gimnasio
(the gym)
el partido
(the game/the match)
la carrera
(the race)
el torneo
(the tournament)
la pelota
(the ball)
el casco
(the helmet)
la red
(the net)
el fútbol
(soccer)
el fútbol americano
(American football)
el béisbol
(baseball)

el golf
(golf)
el baloncesto
(basketball)
el tenis
(tennis)
el voleibol
(volleyball)

Scenario #1 - Trying Out For the Races

Gael: *Creo que me uniré a la competencia de la escuela.*
(I think I'll join the school's competition.)

Ruben: *¿Qué competencia?*
(What competition?)

Gael: *La carrera entre los alumnos de décimo y undécimo grado.*
(The race between the students from 10th and 11th grade.)

Ruben: *¿Cúal es el premio por ganar?*
(What's the prize for winning?)

Gael: *Un día de películas — pizzas y soda también.*
(A movie day — pizzas and soda, too.)

Ruben: *¿Y solo tenemos que correr y vencer a los estudiantes de décimo grado?*
(And we only have to run and beat the 10th graders?)

Gael: *¡Si! Eso es todo. Me inscribiré en la carrera y comenzaré a practicar corriendo por el vecindario.*

(Yes! That's all. I'll sign up for the race and start practicing running around the neighborhood.)

Ruben: *¡Quiero registrarme también!*
(I want to sign up too!)

Gael: *¡Inscribámonos juntos! Nos aseguraremos de ganar el día de películas.*
(Let's sign up together! We'll make sure to win the movie day.)

Ruben: *Suena como un gran plan.*
(Sounds like a great plan.)

Gael: *Incluso podríamos practicar corriendo en el campo de la escuela.*
(We could even practice running in the school's field.)

Ruben: *¡Hagamoslo!*
(Let's do it!)

Scenario #2 - A Friendly Match

Jessica: *¿Quieres jugar baloncesto conmigo después de la escuela?*
(Do you want to play basketball with me after school?)

Katy: *¿No deberíamos hacer nuestra tarea a esa hora?*
(Shouldn't we do our homework at that time?)

Jessica: *Será un partido rápido. Todavía me duele de cuando me venciste la semana pasada.*
(It'll be a quick match. I'm still sore from when you beat me last week.)

Katy: *Supongo que soy mejor en balencesto.*
(I suppose I'm better at basketball.)

Jessica: *¡Pruébalo entonces! Hagamos sola una ronda para que podamos terminar nuestro trabajo.*

(Prove it then! Let's do just one round, so we can finish our work.)

Katy: *Suena divertido — es un partido.*
(Sounds fun — it's a match.)

Jessica: *Necesito que sepas que yo voy a ganar.*
(I need you to know that I'm going to win.)

Katy: *¡Ja-ja! Ahí veremos.*
(Ha-ha! We'll see.)

Jessica: *¡Si! Lo haremos.*
(Yes! We will.)

Katy: *Nos vemos a las tres de la tarde entonces.*
(I'll see you at 3:00 PM then.)

Scenario #3 - The Watch Party

Javier: *Dana y yo tendremos una fiesta esta noche para ver el partido de fútbol entre Cánada versus Francia. Deberías venir.*
(Dana and I are having a party tonight to watch the soccer match between Canada and France. You should come.)

Kriss: *Me encantaría ir. ¿A qué hora comienza?*
(I'd love to go. At what time does it start?)

Javier: *Comenzará a las siete y media de la noche.*
(It'll start at 7:30 PM.)

Kriss: *¡Perfecto! Ahí estaré.*
(Perfect! I'll be there.)

Javier: *Traé tu jersey canadiense si tienes una. Esta noche, estaremos apoyando al equipo canadiense.*
(Bring your Canadian jersey if you have one. Tonight, we'll be rooting for the Canadian team.)

Kriss: *¡Lo haré!*

(I'll do it!)

4.7 The Arts

Art is both subjective and powerful. Artistic expression allows humanity to articulate its existence and emotions through colors and shapes and sounds. From paintings, sculptures, drawings to movies, books, and performances, art speaks volumes from the depths of the mind. Art can be shocking and inspiring. Other times, it may be frightening and complex. Any canvas, be it a sheet of paper, an empty camera roll, or a slab of ceramic, can become an explosion of truth and metaphor, waiting to be desired. Spanish culture doesn't lack monumental artists; the likes of Gabriel García Márquez, the Colombian writer, and Pablo Picasso, the Spanish painter, are just a couple of artists from an extensive list of greats. In this section, we will explore important terms and phrases that relate to the field of arts. The table below will highlight important vocabulary words to know. Example scenarios will place the phrases and terms into context after the table.

The Beauty of the Arts

The table below features some necessary terms and phrases to know when discussing art-related topics. These words may have appeared in previous sections, but it's still necessary to emphasize their importance:

Art Terms
el arte   (art)
un artista   (an artist)
una obra de arte   (artwork)

un dibujo
(a drawing)
una pintura
(a painting)
fotografía
(photography)
una escultura
(a sculpture)
la técnica
(the technique)
la textura
(the texture)
una cámara
(the camera)
una fotografía
(a photograph)
la estética
(the aesthetics)
un lienzo
(a canvas)
cerámica
(ceramics)

una colección
(a collection)
el muséo
(the museum)
un escritor/una escritora
(a writer/a writer (feminine))
una historia
(a story)
un libro
(a book)
un director/una directora
(a director/a director (feminine))
un actor/una actriz
(an actor/actress)
una película
(a movie)
un cine
(a movie theater)

Scenario #1 - A Day at the Museum

Roberto: *¿A qué museo prefieres ir hoy: el Museo Metropolitano de Arte o el Museo de Arte Moderna?*
(To which museum do you prefer going to today: the Metropolitan Museum of Art of the Museum of Modern Art?)

Madeline: *Prefiero ir al Museo de Arte Moderna. Quiero ver pinturas de Vincent Van Gogh.*
(I'd rather go to the Museum of Modern Art. I want to see paintings by Vincent Van Gogh.)

Roberto: *El Museo de Arte Moderna tiene toda una colección de penturas hechas por Van Gogh.*
(The Museum of Modern Art has an entire collection of paintings done by Van Gogh.)

Madeline: *¡Eso es muy emocionante! También quiero ver obras de arte por Andy Warhol.*
(That's so exciting! I also want to see works of art by Andy Warhol.)

Roberto: *El museo también tiene una colección de Warhol. La he visto, es enorme.*
(The museum also has a collection by Warhol. I've seen it; it's huge.)

Madeline: *¿Podríamos ir a un museo de fotografía por la noche?*
(Could we go to a photography museum at night?)

Roberto: *Sí, hay varios en Manhattan. Hasta podríamos ir al Museo de Brooklyn y ver la exposición de fotografía.*
(Yeah, there are many in Manhattan. We could even go to the Brooklyn Museum and look at the photography exhibit.)

Madeline: *Me gusta esa idea.*
(I like that idea.)

Roberto: *¡Hagámoslo!*

(Let's do it!)

Madeline: *Vamos.*
(Let's go.)

Scenario #2 - A Movie Night

Natalie: *Vi en el internet que la película que vamos a ver hoy no es muy buena.*
(I saw online that the movie that we're going to watch today isn't very good.)

Debra: *¿Por qué dice la gente que es una película mala? Es hecha por el director que a ganado varios premios.*
(Why do people say it's a bad movie? It's made by the director who has won multiple awards.)

Natalie: *Mucha gente dijo que la película realmente no tiene una trama.*
(A lot of people said that the movie doesn't really have a plot.)

Debra: *Que extraño...¿Siempre la quieres ver?*
(That's strange. Do you still want to watch it?)

Natalie: *Sí, no tengo ni un problema. Si termina siendo una película mala, por lo menos pudimos descansar un poco.*
(Yes, I don't have a problem. If it ends up being a bad movie, at least, we got to rest for a bit.)

Debra: *Tienes razon. Ya compramos los boletos y todo. Y una actriz que a mi me encanta también es parte del grupo de actores en la película.*
(You're right. We already bought the tickets and everything. And an actress whom I love is also part of the movie's cast.)

Natalie: *Muy bién, vamos.*
(Alright, let's go.)

4.8 Science & Technology

Science is the study of the natural world; technology is humanity's solution to boost and enhance our place in the natural world. In the last 250 years, human beings have been able to discover so much insight and advancements because of scientific study. Vaccines, space exploration, computers, automated robots, and driverless cars — the accomplishments have and will continue to accumulate. But, humanity faces new challenges that will demand revolutionary solutions to maintain stability for our kind. Intriguingly, Spanish culture contains some amazing scientific figures, such as Santiago Ramón y Cajal, one of the earliest experts in neuroscience, and Luis Federico Leloir, a biochemist who uncovered mysteries regarding metabolic mechanisms in the body. In this section, we will explore the important terms and phrases that relate to the field of science. The table below will highlight important vocabulary words to know, and the example scenarios will place the phrases and terms into context.

Scientific Wonders

The table below features some necessary terms and phrases to know when discussing science-related topics.

Science Terms
la ciencia   (science)
la ciencias de la vida   (life sciences)
las ciencias físicas   (physical sciences)
un científico   (a scientist)

un organismo
(an organism)
la energía
(energy)
biología
(biology)
astronomía
(astronomy)
física
(physics)
química
(chemistry)
la tecnología
(technology)
un robot
(a robot)
la memoria
(memory)
la privacidad
(privacy)
la red
(network)
máquinas
(machines)

Scenario #1 - A Lunar Discovery

Edward: *Mamá, ¿qué es eso?*
  (Mom, what's that?)

Maria: *Esa es la luna. Es parte de la tierra.*
  (That is the moon. It's part of the Earth.)

Edward: *¿Y qué es la luna?*
  (And what is the moon?)

Maria: *Es un satélite natural y gira alrededor de la tierra.*
  (It's a natural satellite, and it rotates around the Earth.)

Edward: *¿De qué está hecha la luna?*
  (What is the moon made out of?)

Maria: *La luna está hecha de rocas y tierra. Los científicos dicen que la luna nació cuando un meteorito golpeó la tierra y toda esas rocas flotantes formaron la luna.*
  (The moon is made up of rocks and dirt. Scientists say that the moon was born when a meteorite hit the Earth and all those floating rocks formed the moon.)

Edward: *¿De dónde vino el meteorito?*
  (Where did the meteorite come from?)

Maria: *Del espacio exterior. Los meteoritos siempre vuelan a través del sistema solar y la galaxia.*
  (From the outer space. Meteorites are always flying across the solar system and the galaxy.)

Edward: *¿Y dónde está la galaxia? ¿Nuestra galaxia?*
  (And where is the galaxy? Our galaxy?)

Maria: *Nuestra galaxia se llama la Vía Láctea y flota dentro del universo.*
  (Our galaxy is called the Milky Way, and it floats inside the universe.)

Edward: *Quiero estudiar la galaxia.*
（I want to study the galaxy).

Maria: *Los científicos que estudian el espacio exterior se llaman astrónomos.*
（The scientists who study outer space are called astronomers.)

Edward: *Yo quiero ser un astrónomo.*
（I want to be an astronomer).

Maria: *Espero que sí, hijo. Vamos, entremos. La noche se está poniendo fría.*
（I hope so, son. Come on, let's go inside. The night is getting chilly.)

Scenario #2 - Favorite Fields

Ced: *¿Cuál era tu materia favorita en la escuela?*
（What was your favorite subject in school?)

Michelle: *Biología. Me encantaba aprender sobre células, animales y biomas.*
（Biology. I loved learning about cells, animals, and biome.)

Ced: *¿Es por eso que te convertiste en bióloga?*
（Is that why you became a biologist?)

Michelle: *Sí ja-ja-ja. Exactamente por eso.*
（Yeah, ha-ha-ha. That's exactly why.)

Ced: *¿En qué rama de la biología te enfocas?*
（What branch of biology do you focus on?)

Michelle: *Me enfoco en biología marina. Estoy realmente interesada en los comportamientos de los animales marinos y sus entornos.*
（I focus on marine biology. I'm really interested in the behaviors of sea animals and their environments.)

Ced: *Eso es muy interesante. ¡Buena suerte en tu futuras investigaciónes!*

(That's very interesting. Good luck on your future research!)

Michelle: *¡Muchas, gracias!*

(Thank you very much!)

Scenario #3 - The Inventor

Daniel: *Estoy construyendo un robot que ayudará a los médicos con cirugías delicadas.*

(I'm building a robot that will help doctors with delicate surgeries.)

Phill: *¿Cómo funciona?*

(How does it work?)

Daniel: *Crea un rayo láser tan fino y tan potente que puede cortar pequeñas porciones de materia. Por ejemplo, tumores y quistes.*

(It creates a laser beam so thin and so potent that it can slice small portions of matter. For example, tumors and cysts.)

Phill: *¡Eso es fenomenal! ¿Cuándo estará listo el primer prototipo?*

(That's phenomenal! When will the first prototype be ready?)

Daniel: *Lo más probable es que en unos cinco meses.*

(Most likely, in about five months.)

Phill: *Te deseo buena suerte con tu proyecto.*

(I wish you good luck on your project.)

Daniel: *Gracias.*

(Thank you.)

4.9 Education, School, & University

Education is an important pillar across all cultures. Educational institutions have existed for thousands of years, seeking to teach and prepare future generations of thinkers and world citizens. In most countries, school is a full-time career for students from age five to the early or mid-twenties. And even then, graduate schools are available to advance the expertise of curious, hard-working minds. Needless to say, education is the foundation of a healthy society; knowledgable citizens will always be ready to defend, protect, and ensure their communities' futures. In this section, we will explore the important terms and phrases that relate to the field of education. The table below will highlight important vocabulary words to know. Following the graphic, example scenarios will place the phrases and terms into context.

Education for All

The table below features some necessary terms and phrases to know when discussing education-related topics.

Educational Terms
la educación   (education)
una escuela   (a school)
un colegio/una universidad   (a college/university)
una clase   (a class/lecture)
la concentración de estudio   (major of study)

académicos
(academics)
un título
(a degree)
un diploma
(a diploma)
la tarea
(homework)
estudiar
(to study)
el profesor/la profesora
(the professor/the professor (feminine))
el maestro/la maestra
(the teacher/the teacher (feminine)
el estudiante/la estudiante
(the student/the student (feminine))
Licensiatura en humanidades/ciencias
(Bachelor of Arts/Sciences)
un certificado
(a certificate)
una carrera
(a career)

Scenario #1 - New University Students

Carl: *¿A qué universidad vas a ir en el otoño?*
(What university are you going to in the fall?)

Maya: *Fui aceptada en la Universidad de Pennsylvania. Estoy empezando las clases en agosto.*
(I was accepted into the University of Pennsylvania. I'm starting classes in August.)

Carl: *¡Eso es genial! Voy a la universidad de Nueva York. Mis clases comienzan a principios de septiembre.*
(That's awesome! I'm going to New York University. My classes start early September)

Maya: *¡Que bien! ¿Qué será tu concentración de estudio?*
(That's great! What's going to be your major?)

Carl: *Historia del arte y voy a sacar un menor en danza. ¿Y tú?*
(Art history and I'm going to take a minor in dance. And you?)

Maya: *Voy a tener dos concentraciones de estudio: matemáticas y ciencias de la computación. Quiero ser una ingeniera informática.*
(I'm going to have two majors: mathematics and computer science. I want to be a computer engineer.)

Carl: *Quiero ser un curador de museo.*
(I want to become a museum curator.)

Maya: *¡Que genial! Estoy segura de que te encantará aprender sobre la historia del arte.*
(That's awesome! I'm sure you'll love learning about art history.)

Carl: *¡Ambos seremos fantásticos!*
(We'll both be fantastic!)

Maya: *¡Sí! Definitivamente.*

(Yes! Definitely.)

Carl: *Bueno, te veo el la clase de ciencia política.*
(Okay, I'll see you in political science class.)

Maya: *Te veo en un rato.*
(I'll see you in a bit.)

Scenario #2 - A New School Year

Melissa: *Jennifer comienza el primer grado la próxima semana. Ella esta tan emocionada.*
(Jennifer starts the first grade next week. She's so excited.)

Sarah: *Qué preciosa. Tobias está comenzando el segundo grado en dos semanas. Él dice que se siente nervioso por comenzar una nueva escuela.*
(She's so precious. Tobias is starting the second grade in two weeks. He says he feels nervous about starting a new school.)

Melissa: *¡Estará bien! Él y Jennifer podrían tener el mismo receso. Estoy segura de que se convertirán en buenos amigos.*

(He'll be fine! He and Jennifer might have the same recess break. I'm sure they'll become good friends.)

Sarah: *Espero que sí. Ya hablé con sus nuevos maestros y me aseguraron que todos los niños son amables y amigables.*
(I hope so. I spoke to his new teachers already, and they assured me that all the kids are kind and friendly.)

Melissa: *Y lo serán. Tobias hará muchos amigos al final del primer día.*
(And they will be. Tobias will make tons of friends by the end of the first day.)

Sarah: *Eso es lo que le dije. Tal vez deberíamos planear una cita de juego entre Jennifer y Tobias para que puedan pasar un poco de tiempo juntos.*

(That's what I told him. Maybe we should plan a playdate between Jennifer and Tobias, so they can spend a bit of time together.)

Melissa: *Deberíamos aprovechar el tiempo ahora antes de que comiencen todos las tareas y los proyectos.*
(We should take advantage of the time now before all the homework and projects begin.)

Sarah: *¡Excelente! Hagámoslo. Este será un gran año escolar nuevo.*
(Great! Let's make it happen. This will be a great new school year.)

Melissa: *Definitivamente. Nuestros dos hijos serán estudiantes maravillosos.*
(Definitely. Both our kids will be wonderful students.)

Chapter 5 - Spanish Phrases IV: Miscellaneous Phrases

5.1 Law & Crime

Laws and social rules exist to protect citizens and institutions. Laws provide order and safety to millions of people; they are created to regulate unwanted, harmful behavior and are reinforced by social and governmental systems. Laws ensure that society functions properly and that the bad ones are removed from the public. No one wants to feel in danger in their own block, neighborhood, or city. Because of that, laws impart security to all Samaritans everywhere. In this section, we will explore important terms and phrases that relate to the field of law and crime. The table below will highlight important vocabulary words to know, and example scenarios will place the phrases and terms into context.

Civil Obedience & Crime

The table below features some necessary terms and phrases to know when discussing law-related topics.

Law Terms
la ley
(the law)
la policia
(the police)
el acusado/la acusada
(the accused/the accused (feminine))
un abogado/una abogada
(a lawyer/a lawyer (feminine))

un juez
(a judge)
el jurado
(the jury)
el tribunal
(the court)
un crimen
(a crime)
una infracción
(an infraction)
arrestar
(to arrest)
el juicio
(the trial)
una multa
(a fine)
Investigar
(to investigate)
apelar
(to appeal)
la prueba
(evidence)

un testigo
(a witness)
la sentencia
(the ruling)
aconsejar
(to advice)

Scenario #1 - Stopped by the Police

Marvin: *Hola, oficial, ¿qué parece ser el problema?*
(Hello, officer, what seems to be the problem?)

Police Officer: *¿Puedo ver su identificación de automóvil, su póliza de seguro de automóvil y su identificación?*
(Can I see your car identification, your car insurance policy, and your I.D.?)

Marvin: *Sí, por supuesto. Aquí tiene todo.*
(Yes, of course. Here you go.)

Police Officer: *Gracias. Lo detuve porque cruzó una luz roja. ¿Se dió cuenta?*
(Thank you. I pulled you over because you crossed a red light. Did you notice?)

Marvin: *No, no me di cuenta. Fue un error honesto.*
(No, I didn't notice. It was an honest mistake.)

Police Officer: *¿Bebió alcohol hoy, señor?*
(Did you drink alcohol today, sir?)

Marvin: *No, no he bebido nada. Nunca bebería y conduciría. Eso es muy peligroso. Realmente no noté la luz roja — me quedé en blanco.*

(No, I haven't drunk anything. I would never drink and drive. That's very dangerous. I genuinely didn't notice the red light — I blanked out.)

Police Officer: *¿Se está quedando dormido en el volante? Sé que es tarde.*
(Are you falling asleep on the wheel? I know it's late.)

Marvin: *Tampoco me estoy quedando dormido. Me siento bien. ¿Cansado? Sí, pero bien.*
(I'm not falling asleep, either. I feel fine. Am I tired? Yes, but I'm fine.)

Police Officer: *Yo entiendo, solo quiero asegurarme de que pueda llegar a casa de manera segura.*
(I understand, I just want to make sure you can get home safely.)

Marvin: *Yo entiendo también. Realmente estoy bien, no hay problema.*
(I understand, too. I really am fine; there's no problem.)

Police Officer: *Muy bien. Desafortunadamente, todavía tengo que darle una multa porque podría haber tenido un accidente si hubieran otros autos en la carretera.*
(Very good. Unfortunately, I still have to give you a ticket because you could've gotten into an accident if there were other cars on the road.)

Marvin: *Sí, yo comprendo — actué imprudentemente.*
(Yes, I get it — I acted recklessly.)

Police Officer: *Aquí está su multa. Y por favor, conduzca con mayor seguridad. Tenga una buenas noches.*
(Here's your ticket. And please, drive more safely. Have a good night.)

Scenario #2 - An Emergency

9-1-1 Dispatcher: *Hola, 9-1-1. ¿Cuál es su emergencia?*
  (Hello, 9-1-1. What's your emergency?)

Glenda: *Sí, hola, hay un intruso en mi patio trasero. Vivo sola y tengo miedo de acercarme a él.*
  (Yes, hello, there's an intruder in my backyard. I live alone, and I'm scared to approach him.)

9-1-1 Dispatcher: *No se acerque a él, señora. Podría tener un arma — no lo sabemos. ¿Qué está haciendo?*
  (Do not approach him, ma'am. He could have a weapon — we don't know. What is he doing?)

Glenda: *El es un hombre adulto. Se durmió debajo de mi arbol de naranjas. Probablemente se subió por mi cerca.*
  (He's an adult man. He fell asleep under my oranges tree. He probably climbed over my fence.)

9-1-1 Dispatcher: *¿Sabe cuánto tiempo ha estado en su propiedad?*
  (Do you know how long he's been on your property?)

Glenda: *No estoy segura. Me acabo de dar cuenta hace unos momentos.*
  (I'm not sure. I just noticed a few moments ago.)

9-1-1 Dispatcher: *De acuerdo, la policía está en camino. Quédese adentro, y si él trata de entrar a su casa, llámenos nuevamente.*
  (Okay, the police are on their way. Stay indoors, and if he tries to go inside your home, call us again.)

Glenda: *Muchas gracias!*
  (Thank you so much!)

5.2 Home & Property

Home is where the heart is, as the saying goes. Most of us are lucky enough to have a warm domicile waiting for us at the end of a long day. Family awaits; the pets await. The home is a special place full of memories and wonderments. A house is not merely a location; it's also a unique setting for brilliance and affection. Other forms of property, like lots and buildings, while less personal, do still offer monetary gains. Everyone wishes to own his or her own land and take part of a fruitful life. In this section, we will explore important terms and phrases that relate to the field of homes and property. The table below will highlight important vocabulary words to know. Following the graphic, example scenarios will place the phrases and terms into context.

Property: The Value of Goods

The table below features some necessary terms and phrases to know when discussing property-related topics.

Property Terms
propiedad
(property)
tierra
(land)
título de propiedad
(land deed)
vender
(to sell)
comprar
(to buy)

un agente de prepiedad
(a property agent)
bienes raíces
(real estate)
una casa/el hogar
(a house/home)
la sala
(the living room)
un cuarto
(a bedroom)
el baño
(the bathroom)
la cocina
(the kitchen)
el sótano
(the basement)
el ático
(the attic)
el patio delantero
(the front yard)

el patio trasero
(the backyard)
los bienes
(the assets)
el área
(the area)
una hipoteca
(a mortgage)
propiedados de vivienda
(homeowner)

Scenario #1 - Selling the House

Ron: *Kim y yo estamos pensando en vender la casa.*
(Kim and I are thinking of selling the house.)

Augosto: *Eso suena muy bien. ¿Están buscando agentes inmobiliarios?*
(That sounds very good. Are you looking for a real estate agent?)

Ron: *Sí, ya comenzamos a buscar uno en por en internet. Queremos una evaluación de nuestra casa antes de pensar en un precio.*
(Yes, we started searching online for one. We want an evaluation of our house before we think of a price.)

Augosto: *¿Y a dónde quieren mudarse?*
(And where do you both want to move to?)

Ron: *Kim quiere mudarse a San Francisco. Pero prefiero mudarme al sur de California. Quizás un lugar como San Diego.*

(Kim wants to move to San Francisco. But I'd rather move to Southern California. Maybe a place like San Diego.)

Augosto: *San Diego es muy agradable. Tienen una casa hermosa, así que estoy seguro de que tendrán los fondos para mudarse a cualquier lugar.*

(San Diego is very nice. You both have a beautiful home, so I'm sure you'll have the funds to move anywhere.)

Ron: *Gracias. Sí, nuestra casa cuenta con cuatro habitaciones, dos baños, una cocina con encimeras de cerámica — es grandísima. No creemos que tengamos problemas para venderla.*

(Thank you. Yeah, our house comes with four bedrooms, two bathrooms, a kitchen with ceramic countertops — it's huge. We don't think we'll have issues selling it.)

Augosto: *Si ambos necesitan ayuda para encontrar un agente inmobiliario que trabaje bien, hágamelo saber. Conozco una agente excelente que me ayudó a comprar mi propiedad en Santa Crúz.*

(If you both need help finding a real estate agent who works great, let me know. I know an excellent agent who helped me buy my Santa Cruz property.)

Ron: *¿La casa frente al mar con las pasarelas de piedra?*
(The beachfront house with the stone walkways?)

Augosto: *Exactamente esa.*
(Exactly that one.)

Ron: *Le diré a Kim. Tal vez la llamaremos.*
(I'll tell Kim. We might give her a call.)

Augusto: *Super, solo házmelo saber.*
(Great, just let me know.)

Scenario #2: The Renovation

Richard: *Quiero conseguir nuevos pisos de madera para la sala.*
> (I want to get new wooden floors for the living room.)

Bella: *Creo que primero deberíamos trabajar en el baño. Ambos queremos nuevas baldosas. Y un nuevo lavabo.*
> (I think we should work on the bathroom first. We both want new floor tiles. And a new sink.)

Richard: *Es verdad. Si obtenemos nuevos pisos de madera, también necesitaríamos comprar nuevos muebles.*
> (That's true. If we get new wooden floors, we would also need to buy new furniture.)

Bella: *Cierto. Comencemos las renovaciones con el baño. Luego podemos pasar a la sala e incluso al dormitorio principal.*
> (True. Let's start the renovations with the bathroom. Then we can move on to the living room and even the master bedroom.)

Richard: *¿De qué color vamos a pintar las paredes del dormitorio?*
> (What color are we going to use to paint the bedroom walls?)

Bella: *Estaba pensando en un azul claro o un lila claro.*
> (I was thinking a light blue or a light lilac.)

Richard: *Ambos suenan hermosos. Pero sí, comenzaremos las renovaciones en el baño.*
> (Both sound beautiful. But yes, we'll start the renovations in the bathroom.)

Bella: *Me encanta.*
> (I love it.)

5.3 Nature, Animals, & Plants

Nature surrounds us. We ourselves are natural beings that rely on natural resources for survival. Past our concrete and glass metropolitan areas, nature resides in calmness and serenity. Since the very beginning, humanity has tried to mold and shape nature to its whims. Even in the last few thousand years, we've domesticated plants and animal species to facilitate our dependence on natural resources. Still, nature is an overwhelming presence that dictates the future of our kind. The world harbors a diverse biosphere that's full of wonders and mysteries; nature itself is a profound entity that will continue to have dominance over us. All we can do is stand back and witness its immensity. In this section, we will explore important terms and phrases that relate to the natural world. The table below will highlight important vocabulary words to know. Following the graphic, example scenarios will place the phrases and terms into context.

Nature: The Living Organism

The table below features some necessary terms and phrases to know when discussing nature-related topics.

Nature Terms
la naturaleza
(nature)
animales
(animals)
plantas
(plants)
un árbol
(a tree)

una flor
(una flor)
un bosque
(a forest)
la montaña
(the mountain)
el clima
(the climate)
la atmósfera
(the atmosphere)
el medioambiente
(the environment)
el tiempo
(the weather)
una nube
(a cloud)
el viento
(the wind)
una tormenta
(a storm)
los insectos
(insects)

las aves
(birds)
la ecología
(the ecology)
animales marinos/animales terrestres
(marine animals/land animals)
el calor/el frio
(the heat, the cold)
el planeta
(the planet)
el Calientamento Global
(Global Warming)

Scenario #1 - Weather Small Talk

Bill: *Se supone que va a nevar este fin de semana.*
  (It's supposed to snow this weekend.)

Oliver: *¿De verdad? Pensé que iba a estar parcialmente nublado.*
  (Really? I thought it was going to be partly cloudy.)

Bill: *El reportero del tiempo dijo que va a nevar seis pulgadas.*
  (The weather reporter said that it's going to snow six inches.)

Oliver: *Este podría ser un buen fin de semana para llevar a mis hijos a la estación de esquí.*
  (This might be a good weekend to take my kids to the ski resort.)

Bill: *Iba a llevar a mis hijos a acampar, pero con ese pronóstico, sería mejor hacerlo la próxima semana.*

(I was going to take my children camping, but with that forecast, it'd be better to do it next week.)

Oliver: *Siempre puedes conseguir una cabaña en el bosque. Los guardaparques siempre se aseguran de que las carreteras de montaña estén despejadas de nieve.*

(You could always get a cabin in the forest. The park rangers always make sure the mountain roads are cleared from snow.)

Bill: *Es verdad. Pero ojalá, no nieve y podamos salir.*

(That's true. But hopefully, it won't snow and we can go out.)

Oliver: *La temporada de invierno es cruel.*
(The winter season is cruel.)

Bill: *¡Sí! El viento se congela, las flores desaparecen y todas las nubes están llenas de nieve.*

(Yes! The wind is freezing, the flowers disappear, and all the clouds are full of snow.)

Oliver: *Ya quiero la primavera.*
(I want Spring already.)

Bill: *¡Yo también!*
(Me too!)

Scenario #2 - A Camping Trip

Jacob: *El lago está muy tranquilo.*
(The lake is very calm.)

Owen: *Sí, se pueden ver a los peces nadando dentro del agua.*
(Yeah, you can see the fish swimming in the water.)

Jacob: *El atardecer también es increíble.*
(The sunset is incredible, too.)

Owen: *Lo es. ¿Crees que volveremos a ver al ciervo?*
(It is. Do you think we're going to see the deer again?)

Jacob: *Creo que sí. Hay una gran población de ciervos en este parque nacional.*
(I think so. There's a large deer population in this national park.)

Owen: *He visto muchos pájaros y un zorro desde que llegamos.*
(I've seen a lot of birds and a fox since we got here.)

Jacob: *La noche va a estar despejada. Estoy seguro de que veremos más animales en la luz de la luna.*
(The night is going to be clear. I'm sure we'll see more animals in the moonlight.)

Owen: *¡No puedo esperar!*
(I can't wait!)

Scenario #3 - A Starry Night

Kai: *La luna se ve masiva a través del telescopio.*
(The moon looks massive through the telescope.)

Iris: *Las estrellas se ven tan brillantes. Nunca he visto tantas a la vez.*
(The stars look so brilliant. I've never seen so many at once.)

Kai: *Venir al cañón fue una gran idea.*
(Coming to the canyon was a great idea.)

Iris: *¡Mira! ¡Una estrella fugaz!*
(Look! A shooting star!)

Kai: *Es tan hermosa. Me alegra que no haga demasiado frío también.*
(It's so beautiful. I'm glad it's not too cold, either.)

Iris: *Yo también. La noche está perfecta.*

(Me too. The night is perfect.)

Kai: *¿Crees que nos encontraremos con algunos coyotes?*
(Do you think we'll run into some coyotes?)

Iris: *No lo creo. Viven más cerca de los ríos.*
(I don't think so. They live closer to the rivers.)

Kai: *Estaré atenta a los animales, por si acaso.*
(I'll be on the lookout for animals, just in case.)

Iris: *Bueno. Buscaré a Saturno con el telescopio.*
(Okay. I'll look for Saturn with the telescope.)

5.4 Set Phrases & Idiomatic Expressions

In this section, we will explore common colloquial terms and phrases spoken by Spanish speakers. The various idiomatic expressions will be accompanied by conversational examples.

Set Phrase	Example
Más ___ que nada (very)	*Este helado es más rico que nada.* (This ice cream is very delicious.)
Tiene pinta de ser (It looks)	*Ese carro tiene pinta de ser nuevo.* (That car looks to be new.)
En mi día a día (usually, often)	*En mi día a día me río mucho.* (Often, I laugh a lot.)
Como ningún otro	*Él me quiere como ningun otro.*

(like no one else)	(He loves me like no one else.)
Desde luego (of course)	*Desde luego que me iré.* (Of course, I'll leave.)
Ganarse la vida (to earn a living)	*Me ganaré la vida vendiendo libro.* (I'll earn a living by selling books.)
Por otra parte (on the other hand)	*Me gustaría ir a la playa, por otra parte, quiero dormir.* (I would like to go to the beach, but on the other hand, I want to sleep.)
Dar vueltas a ____ (Overthinking something)	*Deja de darle vueltas al tema de la comida.* (Stop overthinking the topic of food.)
Poner en marcha (to set forth a plan)	*Poneremos en marcha el plan de comprar una computadora nueva.* (We'll set forth a plan to buy a new computer.)
el temaso (the greatest song)	*La nueva canció es un temaso.* (The new song is the greatest song.)

Ir de mochilero (to go backpacking)	*Roberto su fue como mochilero a Peru.* (Roberto left to go backpacking in Peru.)
Un lugar de lujo (a fancy place)	*El nueve restaurante italiano por el río es un lugar de lujo.* (The new Italian restaurant by the river is a fancy place.)
Nunca lo pensé (I've never thought it)	*Nunca lo pensé que pude ir otra vez a la escuela cuand era joven.* *(I never thought that I could've gone to school when I was young.)*
Me lavo las manos (I wash my hands of this)	*Me labo las manos del problema enter Marcos y Julian.* (I wash my hands of the problem between Marcos and Julian.)
Un gajo de ____ (a slice of)	*¿Puédo tener un gajo de pastel?* (Could I have a slice of cake?)
Un calor infernal (infernal heat)	*En julio siempre hace un calor infernal.* (In July, there's always an infernal heat.)
Una lluvia torrencial	*Anoche hubo una lluvia*

(torrential rain)	*torrencial en el valle.* (Last night there was torrential rain in the valley.)
Un sol cegado (a bright sun)	*El sol cegado no me dejo manejar correctamente.* (The bright sun didn't let me drive correctly.)
Un diente de ajo (a garlic clove)	*La receta requiere un diente de ajo.* (The recipe requires a garlic clove.)
No tener pelos en la lengua (to be straightforward)	*Sandra es demasiada honesta. Nunca tiene pelos en la lengua.* (Sandra is too honest. She's always straight forward.)
Tirar la casa por la ventana (to spare no expense)	*Tiré la casa por la ventana cuando me compré mi nueva chaqueta.* (I spared no expense when I bought my new jacket.)
Quedarse de piedra (to feel shocked)	*Me quedé de piedra cuando conocí en novio de Ana.* (I felt shocked when I met Ana's new boyfriend.)
De película	*La torta que coninó mi novia fue de película.*

(so good that it's famous)	(The pie that my girlfriend made was so good; it's famous.)
Se me hace agua la boca (mouthwatering)	*Cuando miré la comida, se me hizo agua la boca .* (When I saw the food, I was mouthwatering.)
Echar agua al mar (doing something pointless)	*Tratando de razonar con el es como echar agua al mar.* (Trying to reason with him is pointless.)
Dar a luz (to give birth)	*Madison dió luz la semana pasada. La niñ se mira identica a ella.* (Madison gave birth last week. The girl looks identical to her.)
De par en par (Wide open; large)	*Su sonrisa era de par en par.* (His smile was wide open.)

Scenario # 1 - An Unfortunate Morning

Selena: *Riel, ¿estás bien?*
(Riel, are you okay?)

Riel: *¡Estoy frito!*
(I'm screwed!)

Selena: *¡Que horrible! ¿Pero por qué?*
(That's horrible! But why?)

Riel: *Olvidé que hoy me tocaba hacer una presentación para el grupo.*
(I forgot it was my turn today to give a presentation to the team.)

Selena: *¿Entonces que vas a hacer? Tu presentación se supone que será en veinte minutos.*
(So what are you gonna do? Your presentation is supposed to be in twenty minutes.)

Riel: *No hay tutía. Voy a disculparme con mi supervisor y preguntarle si puedo reprogramar.*
(There is no solution. I'm going to apologize to my supervisor and ask if I can reschedule.)

Selena: *Eso es lo mejor que puedes hacer.*
(That's the best you can do.)

Riel: *Me siento muy avergonzado.*
(I feel so embarrassed.)

Selena: *Parte de la vida – vives y aprendes.*
(Part of life. You live, and you grow.)

5.5 Set Proverbs & Sayings

In this section, we will explore common proverbs and sayings spoken by Spanish speakers. The various proverbial expressions will be accompanied by conversational examples.

El mundo es un pañuelo

(it's a small world)

Brenda: *Fredd, ¿alguna vez conociste a Daisy McNeil?*
(Fredd, have you ever met Daisy McNeil?)

Fredd: *Por supuesto, ella fue mi vecina durante ocho años.*
(Of course, she was my neighbor for eight years.)

Brenda: *¡Qué! Ella ha sido mi compañera de trabajo durante los últimos cinco años.*
(What! She's been my coworker for the last five years.)

Fredd: *¿En serio?*
(Seriously?)

Brenda: *Sí. No puedo creer que la conozcas.*
(Yes. I can't believe you know her.)

Fredd: *El mundo es un pañuelo. Todos conocen a todos.*
(It's a small world. Everyone knows everyone.)

Brenda: *Realmente que lo es.*
(It truly is.)

A lo pecho, hecho

(what is done is done)

Kyle: *¿Acabas de comer mi almuerzo?*
(Did you just ate my lunch?)

Luisa: *¿Ese era tuyo? Pensé que era el mío. ¡Lo siento mucho!*
(Was that one yours? I thought it was mine. I'm so sorry!)

Kyle: *No te preocupes por eso. A lo pecho, hecho.*
(Don't worry about it. What is done is done.)

Luisa: *¿Puedo comprarte un nuevo almuerzo? Es lo menos que puedo hacer.*
(Can I buy you a new lunch? It's the least that I can do.)

Kyle: *Sí puedes. Solo ten más cuidado la próxima vez.*
(Yes, you can. Just be more careful next time.)

Luisa: *¡Lo seré! Vamos a conseguirte otra hamburguesa y papas fritas.*
(I will be! Let's go get you another burger and fries.)

Kyle: *¡Bueno!*
(Okay!)

Cuentas blancas, amistades largas

(overcoming problems lead to long friendships)

Ricardo: *Ayer hablé con Manuel. Me disculpé por tomar todo el crédito por nuestro proyecto conjunto.*
(Yesterday, I spoke to Manuel. I apologized for taking all the credit for our joined project.)

Ricky: *¿Qué te dijo cuando te disculpaste con él?*
(What did he say when you apologized to him?)

Ricardo: *Dijo que necesita tiempo para sanarse del enojo que tiene conmigo.*
(He said he needs time to heal from the anger he has with me.)

Ricky: *Él tiene todo el derecho de sentirse molesto.*
(He has every right to feel upset.)

Ricardo: *Sí, él tiene el derecho. Solo espero que mi comportamiento no arruine nuestra amistad.*

(Yes, he does have a right. I just hope that my behavior doesn't ruin our friendship.)

Ricky: *Es mejor superar el conflicto que huir de él. Ya sabes el dicho: cuentas blancas, amistades largar.*

(It's better to overcome conflict than to flee from it. You know the saying: overcoming problems lead to longer friendships)

Ricardo: *Es verdad. Si superamos este problema, ambos seremos mejores amigos.*

(That's true. If we overcome this issue, we'll both be better friends.)

Ricky: *Solo dale más tiempo.*
(Just give him more time.)

Ricardo: *Lo haré.*
(I will.)

A caballo regalado, no se le miran los dientes

(don't criticize a gift or good wishes)

Consuela: *¿Cómo estuvo la fiesta de cumpleaños de tu hermana?*

(How was your sister's birthday party?)

Mirián: *Fue interesante. Después de darle su regalo, ella se enojó conmigo.*

(It was interesting. After I gave her her gift, she got angry at me.)

Consuela: *Eso es tan raro. ¿Y por qué ella se enojó?*
(That's so strange. And why did she get angry?)

Mirián: *Porque ella dijo que no quería que le dieran ropa.*
(Because she said she didn't want me to give her clothes.)

Consuela: *¿Qué quería en vez?*
(What did she want instead?)

Mirián: *Ella quería tarjetas de regalo para su tienda favorita. Entonces me dijo que odiaba mi regalo.*
(She wanted gift cards to her favorite store. So she told me she hated my gift.)

Consuela: *¿Y qué le dijiste cuando actuó así?*
(And what did you say to her when she acted like this?)

Mirián: Que *al caballo regalado, no se le miran los dientes. Que siempre debes estar agradecido por los regalos de los demas.*
(Don't criticize a gift. You should always be thankful for presents that others give you.)

Consuela: *Estoy segura de que esto será una buena lección de vida para ella.*
(I'm sure that this will be a good life lesson for her.)

Mirián: *También estoy segura. Luego me llamó disculpándose por actuar tan terriblemente.*
(I'm sure, too. She called me later apologizing for acting so awfully.)

Consuela: *¡Crecimiento personal!*
(Personal growth!)

Hablar hasta por los codos

(talk someone's ear off)

Lida: *Si ves a Marisol, andá hacia el otro lado.*
(If you see Marisol, go the other way.)

Samuel: *¿Pero por qué?*
  (But why?)

Lida: *Acaba de regresar de su viaje en las Islas Canarias. Si ella te ve, no dejará de hablar de sus vacaciones.*
  (She just returned from her trip in the Canary Islands. If she sees you, she won't stop talking about her vacation.)

Samuel: *¿Y tiene tanto que decir?*
  (And does she have that much to say?)

Lida: *Te va hablar hasta por los codos. Nadie la podrá detener.*
  (She'll talk your ear off. No one will be able to stop her.)

Samuel: *Gracias por hacérmelo saber. Mantendré mi distancia.*
  (Thanks for letting me know. I'll keep my distance.)

Lida: *Ni un problema.*
  (Not a problem.)

Conclusion

Thank you for reaching the end of the book. *Spanish Grammar for Beginners* is an eclectic language guide; from its genesis, this Spanish-learning book was meant to be both educational and dynamic. It is educational because language learning is a difficult process that requires work, determination, and tenacity. But, with the right resources, such as this guide, learning Spanish can be facilitated and streamlined.

The book was also meant to be dynamic because the language lessons needed to mirror the real world. Spanish is a beautiful, complex language that is spoken by hundreds of millions of people. Spanish does not exist in a vacuum, and thus, this guide needed to feature meaningful lessons, impactful explanations, and detailed conversational scenarios to bring the world of Spanish to your fingertips. Spaniards and Latin Americans might have different ways of speaking, not to mention accents and syntaxial structures, but Spanish is Spanish.

The Spanish lessons and exercises featured in this guide were created to ease any tension and fear and allow the learning to occur. From colors, numbers, and grammar rules to conjugation guides, financial terms, and greetings, *Spanish Grammar for Beginners* offers an extensive and carefully design exploration of the Spanish language. This book can be utilized as many things: a practice workbook, a language guide, reading practice, and even an encyclopedia of Spanish proverbs and colloquialisms. The lessons are repeatable, and you can go at your own pace every single time.

It's important to remember that while mastering a language may seem difficult in the beginning, its tools like the ones in this book enhance any learning experience into an unforgettable language adventure.

Description

In the world, there are twenty countries that use Spanish as their official language, including Mexico, Colombia, and Spain. There are 400 million Spanish speakers worldwide, making it the second most popular language in the globe, second only to Chinese languages. In the United States alone, there are 52 million native Spanish speakers, and the statistics are projected to rise in the next few decades. In a time where Spanish is such a global language, why stay behind, speaking only one language? If you think it's time to learn Spanish, *Spanish Grammar for Beginners* is the perfect language guide you've been searching for.

With *Spanish Grammar for Beginners,* learning Spanish will be easy and fast. Many Spanish guides available online may be outdated and complicated; learning a new language requires great amounts of patience, persistence, and perseverance, so why seek out resources that will not help you in your Spanish-learning journey? *Spanish Grammar for Beginners* is an exciting, lively Spanish guide that features more than thirty Spanish lesson and tons of exercises. The lessons feature a myriad of topics, from understanding fundamental Spanish grammar to becoming familiar with Spanish greetings and language etiquette. Other lessons include learning how to ask for directions, telling time and dates, expressing feelings and emotional states, being able to order food, understanding Spanish proverbs and colloquialisms, and so much more!

Spanish, like most languages in the world, evolves over time. Words and meanings and phrases gain and lose meanings, or gain and lose popularity. It's essential for language guides to remain as current and dynamic as the language itself. It's because of this that *Spanish Grammar for Beginners* offers extensive lessons that reflect the vibrant nature of Spanish. After going over and understanding Spanish grammar, such as conjugations and gendered parts of speech, the following chapters provide example scenarios that also range in topics and conversational complexity. The example scenarios take abstract concepts like Spanish pronouns and vocabulary words and place them into a familiar context. Observe as couples, parents, classmates, co-workers, neighbors, friends, and strangers communicate with one another. Spanish lessons come to life in this book, which will only further enhance the learning experience.

With *Spanish Grammar for Beginners,* you'll gain access to over 140 pages of comprehensive, hands-on instructions to learn and master speaking, understanding, reading, and writing in Spanish. This book will provide you with crucial language learning tips that will positively impact your relationship with *Español.* Quickly learn to grasp the language, and in no time, you'll be capable of constructing your own Spanish phrases. Whether you are traveling to Costa Rica, transferring to a new job in Spain, or starting a study abroad program in Uruguay, *Spanish Grammar for Beginners* will become your ultimate resource. Get started by getting this book today!

Inside you will find:

- *Comprehensive and easy Spanish grammar lessons*
- *Useful grammar tips and tricks to facilitate the Spanish-learning process*
- *Vast selection of topics, ranging from asking directions to expressing common greetings*
- *Over 30+ Spanish lessons with verb, noun, and expression tables*
- *Real-life example conversations to solidify abstract vocabulary*
- *Cultural understandings of Spain and Latin American countries*
- ***And so much more...***

CPSIA information can be obtained
at www.ICGtesting.com
Printed in the USA
BVHW062249060221
599461BV00010B/1051